Joel Goldsmith and I

The inside story of a relationship with a modern mystic

*by*
*Walter Starcke*

*Published by*
*Guadalupe Press*
*P.O. Box 865*
*Boerne, Texas 78006*

ISBN 0-929845-08-0

# JOEL GOLDSMITH

## AND

# I

*The inside story of a realtionship with a mordern mystic*

*by*

## Walter Starcke

Ⴒ

*Today I am a teacher revealing truth, but if tomorrow I should do what we call "die" and my physical presence should leave this world, that would not remove me. I would still be here. What is done with my body would make very little difference because the I of me would still be here and could still teach if only those reaching out for that teaching can realize that there is no death and that we are separated from physical sight but not from actual communion.*

Joel S. Goldsmith, *A Parenthesis in Eternity*

Joel S. Goldsmith and Walter H. Starcke, 1953

# Foreword

$T$his is more than the story of an extraordinary, powerful, and complex spiritual master, Joel S. Goldsmith, and his eighteen-year influence in personally molding my consciousness from the time that I was an eager young man. It also reflects archetypal patterns that through the ages have been present in most father-son or student-teacher relationships. Beneath the surface this tale also illustrates the evolving, changing, and expanding nature of consciousness as it is passed on from generation to generation.

Joel Goldsmith died in 1964. At that time I knew without a doubt that I was to remain silent about my personal relationship with him and not be involved in or identify myself with his teaching and his extensive following. Until now those restrictions have by and large remained in place, apart from the fact that in each of the six books I have written since Joel passed on I have mentioned that he was my most significant teacher. On the other hand, Joel's influence has been so profound in conditioning my consciousness that except for a few significant differences it is impossible for me to know where his consciousness stops and mine begins.

Before telling the story, I want to reiterate my debt of gratitude for the spiritual metamorphosis that Joel instigated in my life. Though I have built on it, added to it, and arrived at some different assumptions, everything I am today and everything I know to be true stems from having personally experienced the divine inner presence that he projected into my consciousness. It has shaped my life. There is no greater gift of love that can be given to a person or received from another than the gift of higher consciousness. Joel's power was not so much in the letter of truth that he spoke but in the transforming mystical power that emanated from his being.

In *Conscious Union with God*, one of Joel's earliest books, he explains:

> *The relationship between teacher and student is a very sacred one and is not dependent upon any degree of human learning that a teacher may possess. Whatever knowledge a spiritual teacher may have acquired will be of very little benefit to his student because what the teacher transmits to the student is his spiritual integrity and uplifted consciousness. Without these he has nothing to give.*

Joel often said that those he loved while in body he would always love. I have personally felt his continued presence in my life for the 40-plus years since he left. My fervent hope is that by the end of this parable the confusing and sometimes painful experiences that I went through with Joel, experiences that bewildered me at the time they occurred, will be seen as Joel's having followed his own spiritual instinct or guidance for a divine purpose.

# Why Now

Twenty-four years after Joel died I was living on a ranch in the Texas Hill Country, nearing the end of a 14-year personal retreat, during which time I did not write or speak in public. For many years a small group known as The Spiritual Frontiers Fellowship continued to ask me to be the keynote speaker at their annual conferences, and each year I refused. Finally, after a number of years, to my own surprise, when they asked me once more I heard myself say that I would. They suggested that if I would also be willing to do a four-day two hour workshop in the afternoons they would be delighted, and when I acquiesced they asked me the title for the workshop. I was surprised, once more, because without thinking I heard myself say it would be on Joel Goldsmith and the Infinite Way.

Those attending the conference were unfamiliar with Joel or his work, which made it necessary for me to some extent define the man as well as his teaching. The impromptu and completely spontaneous talks were recorded, and that resulted in an unrehearsed series of tapes that were made available to a few on my mail list, but not the general public. Nevertheless, after that one exception I still felt strongly that I was not to publicly make any more than casual references to Joel.

After 41 years of refusing to talk about Joel's personal life, another surprising thing happened. The author, Catherine Ponder, whose writings and knowledge of the principles inherent in metaphysics have impacted the entire movement and who is well versed in the lives and writings of the leaders of the past century, including Joel Goldsmith, called me up. Ponder has a set of the original tapes that I had made about my experiences with Joel and has played them off and on over the years. She called to tell me that she felt the time had come for me to make a book out of them. She pointed out that after all this time and without any organization 35 or more of Joel's books are still in print, that hundreds of thousands had sold, and that he is often quoted in *Science Of Mind* and other periodicals, yet no one knows anything about the man himself or how he responded in a one to one relationship. Ponder felt that if I told Joel's and my personal story it would help others better understand his message and avoid possible pitfalls.

After hearing Ponder's advice, something clicked inside of me. Whereas I had always felt I should remain silent, this time it reversed, and though I was not yet fully convinced that I was to tell our story, to some extent the inner ban I had felt for so many years lifted, almost as though Joel was giving me permission to go ahead. And then I received another unexpected nudge.

Out of the blue, I got a call from a highly respected teacher of Joel's work, a man of integrity who has given hundreds of classes on the Infinite Way material, though strictly quoting the writings and tape recordings rather than offering his personal interpretation. I knew this gentleman slightly and had only been in his presence one time about ten years before and had not corresponded with him. He asked me if he and his wife could come visit me from their home on the East coast. He explained that they had something they wanted to tell me. Naturally, if they wanted to come all this way I agreed to see them. When they arrived they told me that they had come because their intuition had told them to and they felt Joel wanted them to urge me to write about my experiences with him and to clarify some of his statements.

There was no way they could have known that I was currently reinterpreting some points in Joel's teaching so that the words he had used at the time would be more in line with what I feel he really meant. At the same time, my inner feelings had a voice of their own. This was no accident. I experienced a kind of psychic excitement as though another dimension of being was breaking through, releasing me to tell our story. Above all, I felt the past rushing into today's awareness, and with it a closeness and love both from and for Joel.

## CHAPTER ONE

# Portraits of the Players

$T$ here were three main characters in this spiritual/ human drama. Joel was the protagonist instigating the plot. John van Druten, who wrote the introduction to Joel's first book, *The Infinite Way*, and who was also instrumental in introducing me to Joel and his teaching, played a key role. I, Walter Starcke, the third player, completed the cast of leading actors in this Trinity-like spiritual relationship.

In order to fully understand how each of us has affected and influenced the plot as it played out, I find it necessary to offer a capsule account of our individual lives up until the time we joined forces and to include a sketch of our appearances and personalities as they were at the time the tale begins.

# Joel

$O$n the surface there is no place where you can separate Joel, the public man, from his teaching. By the time he was well into mid-life he had carefully developed an outer persona that was as impersonal and impervious as the message he taught. Behind his carefully crafted, appealing, easily accessible, and seemingly unruffled and authoritative exterior was a world of personal feelings and a constant sense of loneliness that few of those who knew him were ever aware of. Most of the clues that define his human nature are found hidden between the lines of his actions and choices.

Joel was born in 1892 on Manhattan Island in a Jewish settlement in Harlem. As a small child he was very sensitive and difficult to handle. There was no middle ground; he expressed his likes and dislikes with equal vigor. Joel once told me that even at the beginning of his life he had a hard time living in this world. He felt out of step with the interests of his schoolmates. His mother said that he cried constantly for the first three years of his life.

Ever since Joel was a child he had a more than average difficulty coping with the dog-eat-dog values of society and a reticence toward forming intimate relationships in both his private life and in the workplace. His need to find an impersonal way to cope with his razor-sharp ability to dissect the human condition and his acute awareness of its shortcomings was the price he paid for bringing forth a teaching that helped him, and therefore others find a satisfactory way to live in our competitive and challenging society. We all tend to offer an outer appearance that overcompensates for the vulnerability we feel within, and Joel was no exception.

Fortunately, Joel had a mother who understood him and, intuiting that her complex and overly sensitive son had some kind of unusual destiny, she interceded for him when others found him difficult to understand or cope with. Joel never showed any greater intimacy and more personal feelings about anyone than he did when he spoke of his mother. In later years Joel expressed the depth of his divine love for his mother by saying, "Being in the presence of God is like being with your mother. You don't go to see her for anything other than to just be in her presence."

As for his father, though Joel respected him, on the few occasions when he mentioned him I felt neither a personal connection nor any hint of his father's personality apart from the fact that Joel, being the elder son, was expected to be second in command. He had a younger brother and sister, but he didn't stay in touch with them and never talked about them or what happened to them.

Even in his early youth, Joel began to have paranormal experiences such as a talent for "fore-vision." Perhaps it was a family inheritance because one day he casually mentioned that Houdini, the famous illusionist, was also a close family member, though I could never get him to elaborate on any of those family connections.

Through the years Joel seldom talked of his pre-cognitive experiences because he didn't want his personal life to overshadow his teaching; however, they started at an early age and were extensive. Ultimately they led to his affinity with a sense of parallel universes or "other world" metaphysical approaches. In *Conscious Union with God* he wrote:

> *There was a time when I did not know how to do this (have fore-vision) and I had some very unpleasant experiences. When I was a youngster, my father was a European traveler and spent much of his time abroad. One day, I went to my mother and said, "Mom, something is wrong in Europe; something is wrong with Pop!" There was nothing we could do about this premonition because all we knew was that Father had just landed in England. But the next day we had a cable from him that he had been on his way to catch the Nottingham express and for the first time in 100 trips he had missed his*

*train. That was the very day the Nottingham express was wrecked and everyone aboard was killed—101 people.*

*There were other experiences of warnings of impending danger as, for example, when I astonished my mother by telling her of a railroad wreck in Connecticut, although neither one of us had any way of knowing whether or not this had happened until it was verified in the paper that night. Later on I often caught a certain signal when someone I knew, someone in the family or a close friend, was about to pass on. I never knew or understood these experiences, nor did I know what to do about them.*

Joel's precognition continued throughout his life. In the mid 1950s I remember him telling me that in one way or another the Third World War would come about because of the Palestinian/Israeli conflict. He said that you couldn't kick people out of their homes and expect them not to retaliate. He saw the situation as being a tinder box that would light a fire between the Arab nations and the West.

Joel's father made his living as a lace salesman, and after he became successful the Goldsmiths moved to a larger and grander apartment on Riverside Drive, east of Harlem. When Joel completed the eighth grade his formal schooling ended and he joined his father in the import business. Every year or so he would accompany his father on trips to Germany to buy lace. Joel had no early religious training because, though his parents were reformed Jews who celebrated the holidays, they did not attend synagogue and didn't discuss religion.

When Joel was only 18 his family arranged a marriage with a Jewish girl they thought would make him a good wife;

however, the marriage was soon annulled and Joel said that it was never consummated. In his later life, Joel had a rather Victorian sense of morality, was pretty closed on the subject of sexual relationships, and I was unable to get him to fill in any of the details of his first marriage. For the next twenty years he was single, though I expect he enjoyed surrounding himself with pretty feminine ladies then just as he did when I knew him.

In the First World War Joel joined the marines. It is hard enough to picture this five-foot-four, curly-haired, citified young Jewish man, neither overtly masculine nor feminine, with his puckish nature and inquisitive mind in the military service at all, most particularly as a marine.

By the time Joel went into the service he had already become a Thirty-Third degree Mason, had read everything he could get his hands on of an esoteric nature, and was already well-versed in the Christian Science teaching. He was always ready to share his theories and beliefs and, as in his later life, he doubtless dominated the conversation. To hear him tell it, even in the service he attracted his fellow marines and backed up his positive approach by quoting the 91st Psalm:

> *He that dwelleth in the secret place of the most High…A thousand will fall at thy side, and ten thousand at thy right hand; but it shall not come nigh thy dwelling.*

Joel used to love going to the theater and opera, playing cards, and gambling at the horse races. He drank, went to night clubs in New York, London, Berlin, and anywhere he might be on his sales trips. He was playing the part of a classic man-about-town, but it was more an act of desperation than enjoyment. Nevertheless, with his sly sense of humor, quick retorts, and challenging nature, I can imagine that on most occasions he was the life of the party. Yet, I know that Joel felt that there had to be more to life than that. That something deep inside of him was driving him to find answers, which he ultimately did through Christian Science.

Joel told two different stories about how he was introduced to Christian Science. One was that his father had become deathly ill on a trip to Europe and a friend of Joel's, who turned out to be a Christian Scientist, suggested that Joel contact a practitioner. Feeling that there would be no harm in it and leaving no stone unturned, Joel agreed to do it. Lo and behold, his father was instantly healed, and that began Joel's search. Elsewhere, Joel reported that he himself had contracted a serious case of tuberculosis and was healed by Christian Science.

Joel didn't do anything half way. He was driven by a passion to learn everything he could about any subject that interested him, and to some extent his insatiable appetite for research was a substitute for forming personal human relationships.

Once Joel became interested in spiritual healing phenomena and the religions of the world, he began to read everything he could get his hands on of a spiritual nature. He investigated the Oriental religions, learned Sanskrit, and became well versed in the teachings of Unity and the other metaphysical sources. However, nothing appealed to him or spoke to him as strongly as Mary Baker Eddy's Christian Science revelation.

After the war, Joel's father's import business ceased to exist, and once more the family was faced with financial problems. Joel went on the road as a salesman for a woman's notions company to help support the family, though his heart was not in it. It was on a selling trip to Detroit that the single most important turning point in Joel's life took place.

Joel had contracted a severe head cold and he looked in the telephone book for a Christian Science practitioner to go to who was close to his hotel. It was a Saturday, and the practitioner he contacted told Joel that he didn't take patients on Saturdays because it was his custom to spend that day in meditation. When Joel appealed to him he acquiesced and invited Joel to join him in meditation. That was Joel's first meditation experience and it was as though lightning struck his psyche. Through that meditation he experienced his inner being in a way he never had before. He was literally blown open by it. He left Detroit the next day, and from then on his life and message were centered on meditation.

That experience in meditation showed Joel the possibility of his achieving freedom from his acute sense of critical judgment. At last he had found the avenue he could travel that would offer some respite from the degrading human condition that had seemed inescapable. When Joel returned to Detroit a year later he tried to look up the practitioner to express his gratitude, but he found that the practitioner was no longer listed in the phone book and Joel never saw or heard of him again.

That visit with the Christian Science practitioner marked the beginning of a contradiction in Joel's life and ultimately a paradox in his teaching. He would often say that immediately after his meditation breakthrough he never again wanted to play cards, drink, or indulge in nightlife as though those appetites could keep one from spiritual fulfillment. For Joel, giving power to those indulgences implies that God is not actually the only power and it also creates a separation between the human and the divine. Rather than subjectively denouncing a dependence on those appetites, denouncing them objectifies them and makes even minor participation seem somehow spiritually immoral.

Finally, in the early 1930s when he was in his late thirties, Joel was working for a company in New York that specialized in women's apparel, notions, and laces. Paraphrasing the different ways Joel tells the story, one day his boss called him in and said, "Joel, you have received twenty-two telephone calls today, twenty for spiritual help, and two for business. Take a look at yourself." In other words, he was fired, and to top it off, the great depression was in full swing and jobs were hard to find.

Joel knew then that without a doubt he had no choice but to dedicate his life to his spiritual work. He often recalled sitting on a park bench flat broke and deciding to become a Christian Science practitioner. He borrowed money and managed to get through Christian Science class teaching in New York, began his practice, and married Rose.

In all, Joel had four wives during his lifetime. Twenty years after his annulled marriage, Joel married Rose Robb, another Christian Scientist. A few years older than Joel, Rose was delicate, fragile, overly sensitive, and completely dedicated to living an absolutely spiritual life.

Joel wasn't one to leave any stone unturned so, to test his principle, three years after he became a practitioner and married Rose, he went right to the source—he moved to Boston to be near the Mother Church. At first he literally almost starved. He had to walk miles to his sparsely furnished office because he didn't have bus fare. After days of intense prayer a revelation of supply and his ultimate mystical message came to him. As a result his practice took off.

In *The Spiritual Journey of Joel Goldsmith*, Lorraine Sinkler quotes Joel as saying his break through came when he thought, "It was revealed to me in my inner work that the I is God. I is Self-maintaining and Self-sustaining. I is the source of supply. So I thought, "Oh, I AM THAT I AM means that I embody supply. I include it. It is embraced within my own being. It does not come to me. It flows out from me." After that he soon became one of the busiest and most successful practitioners in Boston. As a result of his popularity it wasn't long before Joel was called before the Board of the Mother Church. They said that because of his Jewish background they wanted to know how he felt about the virgin birth and the Immaculate Conception. He replied, "Oh I believe it. After all, if it is true about me, it must have been true about Jesus," meaning that every birth is virginal and immaculate. Joel did have a tantalizing sense of humor. The Board must have taken it in the right way because he was made First Reader in the Third Church of Christ Scientists in Boston.

Ten years after Joel and Rose went to Boston, Rose became ill and was advised to move to a warm climate, so Joel left his highly successful practice and they moved to Florida. Before Joel had time to build another practice there, Rose died and Joel returned to Boston. It was then that he became embroiled in a painful experience that reinforced his practice of putting as much distance between himself and human nature or the personal side of life as was possible.

Joel and Rose had not made out a will and her children from a previous marriage sued Joel for her estate. He lost the case and with it his entire bank account. Once more Joel was broke. Knowing Joel as I did, his having to go to court must have torn him to pieces and reinforced his desire to have as little to do with the human scene as possible. From then on he always advised his followers never to go to court, and he made himself the promise that he wouldn't either.

Though Joel worked night and day to build up his practice in Boston once more, after all that had happened he couldn't get his heart into it and opened himself to a change. While on a visit to California, a successful Christian Science practitioner in Hollywood asked him to stay there and take care of his practice while he took a year's sabbatical. Joel agreed and settled in. After the year was over the practitioner returned and saw how happy his people were with Joel. He decided to retire and turned his entire practice over to Joel. As his practice grew, Joel's clients wanted more than just his practitioner work; they also wanted teaching. As a result he began to send out an unofficial spiritual message/letter to his practitioner clients, which ultimately led to his conflict with Christian Science headquarters and with the emergence of his own voice.

Joel gave me a collection of those letters. The early ones were more mental and absolute than mystical and had that uniquely Christian Science sound. He would quote Mary Baker Eddy over and over, give her total credit for his beliefs, and set his own opinions aside. In these early letters he would often give page and paragraph in *Science and Health* that backed up his statements. He would say that if we carefully studied Mrs. Eddy's writings we would see the true law with regard to God as the only Cause, and therefore good as the only effect, that evil resulting from the action of the human mind or from evil thoughts was impossible.

Joel quoted page 415:1-3 of *Science and Health* where Mrs. Eddy said, "Immortal Mind is the only cause; therefore disease is neither a cause nor an effect." He points out that in *No and Yes* 10:27 Mrs. Eddy said "Eternal harmony, perpetuity, and perfection constitute the phenomena of being, governed by the immutable and eternal laws of God; whereas matter and human will, intellect, desire, and fear are not the creators, controllers, nor destroyers of life or its harmonies."

Bit-by-bit Joel's letters to his patients stopped quoting Mary Baker Eddy, and his language became less-and-less sounding like *Science and Health* and more and more what eventually became the language of *The Infinite Way*. Though he had not yet dropped the Christian Science use of the word "Mind" as a synonym for God, which he did do before long, his suggestion that there was time to go beyond treatment, affirmations, and denials was enough for the organization to feel he was straying from their doctrine—and he was.

In his later letters he would continue to capitalize the word, "Mind," and tell his readers to let this Mind be in them, which was also in Christ Jesus. Because this Mind was already their mind, they need "take no thought" for health, wealth, peace or harmony. He would tell them to rest in the truth that their Mind is the Truth, the Life, the Principle and Soul of their being and body. Only by resting in this consciousness are they letting this Mind be all things to them.

Joel pointed out that it is natural that we would be tempted to think something; know the truth about something, or make affirmations and denials, because those were the first steps anyone goes through to be born in the new world of spirit. He said those steps had their place but that now the call had come to rise to a higher understanding, implying that he would personally take his students there. No wonder the Christian Science leaders wanted to rein him in. When he added that as God is the Mind of the individual there is no need for words, formulas, prayer, or treatment, he was in violation of the church's advocacy of mental treatment, and that had to be stopped.

During this same time Joel had established a close relationship with the playwright John van Druten, whose biographical sketch follows Joel's. As John had no previous knowledge of the metaphysical approach, Joel tailored his correspondence with him in a less traditionally spiritual-sounding language. The following are in substance two letters Joel wrote to van Druten in August and September of 1945, which hinted at an impending change in his relationship with the Christian Science organization and were about as personal as Joel would get with anyone.*

In the first letter, Joel said that he didn't want to take sides but pointed out that Dr. De Lange, who was a popular teacher of that time, had buckled to the pressure of threats to stop his being a teacher. He pointed out that Laird, another popular teacher, would not back off and was put on probation, and that the Trustees and Directors were threatening lawsuits. He said that it was hard for him to not take sides as he felt that Mrs. Laird represented the height of Christian Science teaching. He claimed that this was an example of how all through history churches or organizations tried to stifle truth.

A month later Joel wrote John a letter showing that the crisis with headquarters had come to him personally and that he wasn't going to sit still for it. Joel wrote that he had just done an article on "healing" which he had written

---

*The law states that the copyrights for letters remain the property of the one who wrote them; however, the letters themselves remain the property of the one who received them. The Goldsmith estate that has the copyrights to Joel's correspondence has not honored my request to quote Joel's letters verbatim; therefore, I will paraphrase a few of those he sent to van Druten and me and come as close as I can to Joel's unique sound and use of language. I have the original letters in my possession to back up the authenticity of the statements and ideas that Joel put forth in them.

right from the shoulder no punches barred. He said that it couldn't be sent out as a letter for "political" reasons but that it was being prepared to go out as a pamphlet in the not too distant future. He said that he would have a few copies made for his inner circle and one would reach John in due time.

When the Mother Church demanded that Joel discontinue sending out letters, it really tore at Joel's soul. After much inner searching, his passion for personal freedom asserted itself and he felt he had no choice but to leave the organization in order to follow his guidance and share his understanding with others. He told me later that if they had allowed him to continue to write his messages he would never have left. Joel then became quite an anathema to the Christian Science organization. Even today many practitioners secretly read Joel's books without publicly acknowledging his work.

When Joel moved to California he met and married his third wife, Nadea, another Christian Science practitioner. She was a rather formidable lady, fairly attractive, but not the typically feminine type that Joel was usually attracted to. She was larger than Joel, friendly, though impersonal, and a bit withdrawn. She seemed to stand aside and observe rather than participate.

Apart from the home he lived in, Joel refused to own any property where he would have to deal with tenants. To keep life as impersonal as possible, he did this because he wanted nothing to do with the business world where personalities were involved, and when he invested it was in impersonal stocks and bonds, mainly utilities and municipal bonds.

Despite the fact that Joel's work involved the lives of thousands, he wanted as little to do with personal contacts as possible. He never had more than one or two employees at a time, and those were always longstanding students whom he felt would disregard his personal-sense-self and see him spiritually.

Joel was himself a contradiction. He was outwardly warm and friendly but at the same time impersonal and detached from human concern. Outwardly his appearance was unimpressive; however, there was a power that emanated from him and something that drew people to him without their understanding why. He spoke softly but everyone would hang on his every word. Just being in his presence made you feel safe and content. Your problems no longer seemed to matter. Fortunately, he was spiritually inspired; otherwise, with his charismatic personality and persuasive personality, he could have been a devilish presence.

Joel's personal life was not without highs and lows. He may have overcome ordinary human needs and desires but in their place he suffered a kind of mystical loneliness. He often said that he longed for just one person who could see him as he really was and yet he made it impossible by advocating total impersonalization. As a case in point, he said, "Do not be concerned about your relationships with people. Consciously maintain your relationship with God, and this will take care of everything else."

Joel's other great anguish was the sense of inadequacy he felt at being unable to share his vision. He voiced his despair in one of the "Wisdoms" that are included at the end of *The Infinite Way*:

> *I have been in deep grief — so intense that it has torn me to pieces inside — and wondered, "Why, O Lord, why?" In the depth of it, the answer has come: the world's inability to receive and respond to this Christ; the rejection of it*

*by these we expect to possess the gift of vision;*
*the gross ignorance and darkness of the human*
*thought. These bounce back upon me — these*
*rejections and this opacity. Give me Grace to rise*
*above my sorrow.*

Joel was no different than any mystical master. Spiritual masters are not born with their haloes. They earn them. Mystics don't come along prepackaged with nice pretty messages they decide to offer the world. They have personal human frustrations and problems that are difficult for them to cope with and in necessarily finding solutions that work for them they come up with answers that they share with others. The price Joel paid in coping with his own inner turmoil translated into the Infinite Way message and became our blessing.

Joel had a passion for freedom. He had an overt desire to free himself and everyone else from all forms of bondage—whether from illness, lack, unsatisfactory personal relationships, or from political domination. That passion for individual freedom became the basis of his life and teaching. In some respects Joel was Moses. He led others to the Promised Land but never quite entered it himself. His passion stood in the way.

# John

Except for the fact that both Joel Goldsmith and John van Druten loved the theater and read voraciously, you couldn't find two people who were less alike. Whereas Joel was short, round, and sporty, John was a rather impressive and dignified figure—over six feet tall. In the early days Joel wore bright plaid sport coats and string ties, looking more like someone you would expect to find at a racetrack than one who would become an outstanding spiritual healer. In contrast, John was sophisticated, and always elegantly groomed. Whereas Joel's speech was tinged with an identifiably New York City intonation, John spoke with a precise, refined, and upper-class English accent. Joel's personality appeared to be outgoing and easily accessible, while John's was relatively introverted and reserved.

John van Druten had a long list of theatrical successes in London and on Broadway as both a playwright and director. His 35-year career, starting in the early 1920s and lasting into the 1950s, included award-winning plays such as *Old Acquaintance, The Voice of the Turtle, I Remember Mama, I Am a Camera,* and *Bell, Book and Candle,* all of which were made into motion pictures. He also wrote a number of screenplays including *Gaslight,* which starred Ingrid Bergman and Charles Boyer, several books, and he directed the original production of Rogers and Hammerstein's musical *The King and I.*

John's father came from a prominent Dutch banking family and his mother from a wealthy, cultured, Dutch/Jewish diamond family. Intermarriages were unacceptable in the 1890s, so his mother and father eloped to England where John was born in 1901. By that time the families had reconciled, and his father soon become the head of an English bank. The van Druten home in London was staffed by a number of servants, including a nanny who taught John to speak French as he was being potty trained.

During the 1920s and 1930s, John was the epitome of a worldly, slightly cynical, well-educated intellectual. He was an extremely well-read man of letters, was fluent in five languages, had excellent tastes in food, wine, and the arts, and was well traveled.

John carried himself with the casual authority of one who was used to being treated with respect. Some say that in his early years he looked like and reminded them of Edward, Prince of Wales, with whom he had dined before Edward abdicated the throne to marry Wally Simpson. Some people thought his manner was aloof and even a bit snobbish, not realizing that he actually cared about what everyone felt. He overcompensated for his deep concern over what everyone thought, particularly about his work. As time went on John became the epitome of a truly gentle man. There was no one in the New York Theater who was more highly respected.

John's friends included all the notable authors, actors, and composers of the day, such as George Bernard Shaw, Noel Coward, Somerset Maugham, Sinclair Lewis, Cole Porter, and Sir Laurence Olivier, to name a few. Aldous Huxley, Christopher Isherwood, and others of the English expatriates living in California were among his literary companions on the West Coast. He had a particularly close relationship with several highly successful women authors of the 1930s and 1940s, including Rebecca West, who wrote a number of successes including *Black Lamb and Grey Falcon* and *The Fountain Overflows,* and Dodie Smith, who wrote several hit plays and the novel, *One Hundred and One Dalmatians,* which was made into a popular movie.

Wanting to please his father, John graduated from university with a law degree. When his father died shortly after John's graduation, having no desire to be a solicitor, he took a job teaching law at a college in Wales where he could travel to London, write theater criticisms for an English language newspaper in Switzerland, and try his hand at playwriting. In 1924 during his first year teaching, he wrote *The Young Woodley,* a play about a student with a crush on his headmaster's wife. Nothing overt happened in the plot, but in those days even mentioning the possibility of a student's having romantic feelings for an older woman would not pass the English censors. Turned down in England, the play was sent to America where it became a smash hit on Broadway. Suddenly, John was making more money in a month than he made all year as a teacher. After the term was over he resigned and made his first voyage to New York where he was warmly received in the top theater circles. That began his love affair with America that resulted in his becoming an American citizen in 1944.

After a number of moderately successful plays, John hit his stride in the 1930s when dramas with strong plot lines were taken over by the motion picture industry and success in the theater depended on an author's ability to write interesting character relationships rather than plots. At the time I met him in 1945, John was the most successful author and director on Broadway, with several plays running simultaneously.

John had been raised with even less religious training than Joel, and he considered himself to be among those sophisticates of the period to whom, as he said, "the most pleasing sound was the sound of falling idols." However, an accident in 1942 led him to search for a spiritual answer.

John was thrown from a horse in Mexico and received a serious arm fracture where the bone broke through the skin. The arm was not properly taken care of and gangrene set in. As a result John had bone deterioration and, being right handed, he not only lost the use of his right arm but was unable to use a typewriter to write his plays. After the medical specialists exhausted their solutions, his seemingly uncorrectable accident caused him, in desperation, to seek help and possibly a healing from a spiritual source.

After searching in a number of directions, an actress friend of John's who was a Christian Scientist urged him to visit a practitioner—that practitioner was Joel S. Goldsmith.

Though John did not receive a miraculous healing from Joel, he was led to read an article about a German physician who had developed a bone graft technique where bone could be taken from one's leg and used to graft a broken arm back together. He went to Germany, had the operation, and it was successful. His right arm ended up being a couple of inches shorter than his left causing him to lean forward slightly when shaking hands. This slight bow-like personal mannerism became one of his signatures.

Because of John's new-found interest in a spiritual approach, his friends, Aldous Huxley, Gerald Heard, and Christopher Isherwood, introduced him to Swami Prabhavananda and the Ramakrishna order of Vedanta. He began to frequent meetings at their temple in Hollywood where a number of intellectuals of that day would gather. He also wrote a number of articles for their publications. One in particular told of a mystical experience he had at breakfast in Schwab's drugstore at which time he said he had experienced the "isness" of the eggs on his plate and felt a sense of the divine presence in everyone in the store.

John was fundamentally an intellectual and his approach to spiritual understanding was through careful analysis and interpretation. His relationship with Goldsmith had a double nature. Joel highly respected John's mind and integrity and he generally spoke to John as an equal with a more careful and intellectually detailed approach than with his other followers. At other times he counseled him as he would any student. His letters to John were far more personal, less cryptic, and of greater length than those he wrote to his other students. For instance, on September 26, 1945, he wrote a letter that sounded as though he was talking to himself.

Joel wrote John that as a celebrity he had to meet things that all those whose heads were stuck above the masses would have to contend with like "self seekers" and "time wasters", and other people's jealousy that had to be dealt with and dispensed. I felt Joel reflected his personal feelings when he added, "The high places, John, are lonely places. Very lonely." He went on to advise John that as he was infinite intelligence itself he would be able to see through it. He said that the way "you disarm the self-seekers is by realizing that a false or negative quality is not the individual but is a universal belief claiming to use the individual as an outlet and use you as a victim or target." Joel told John to impersonalize the ignorance and to see the individual as he would see himself, and when he did he would find completeness in himself. When he added "Greatness walks alone," I felt he was once more talking to himself. He then advised John that if he handled this problem correctly he would draw to himself kindred souls, "at least those of your own level of consciousness."

John kept an apartment in Hollywood at the fashionable Chateau Marmont and he had a date-and-corn farm in the desert between Palm Springs and the Salton Sea. Apart from the ranch manager and the family who worked the ranch, John, a butler, and cook would arrive in January and stay until the end of June when the heat became unbearable. His ranch was below sea level and he often said that a most depressing title for his autobiography would be, "I Live Thirty Feet Below Sea Level."

# Walter

$\mathcal{M}$y German great-great-grandparents on my mother's side came to Texas from Germany in the 1820s when it was still part of Mexico, and bought a sixty thousand-acre land grant family ranch. My great-grandmother, who was born the year Texas became independent, would tell me about small bands of Indians coming around the home that was built fort-like out of blocks of limestone, with small defendable windows on the first floor and wider open ones on the second. My other German ancestors came during the rest of the nineteenth century. Though I think of myself as a fifth generation Texan, I came into this world at Ocean View, Virginia, in 1921 by accident. During the First World War my father served in the army as a dental surgeon. At the end of the war he was stationed in Virginia and stayed there long enough for me to be born before his release and return to Texas.

As I grew up, my upper-middle class background fell somewhere between John's and Joel's. We lived in the so-called "better residential" part of San Antonio where my father practiced dental surgery, had a live-in servant, a new car every year or so, and had joined the Country Club just before my father died of cancer at age 39.

As a child I had a vivid imagination and felt equally at home in both the fantasy and the real worlds. There was always something attracting me to what I now know was an awareness of the spiritual nature of life. I was a happy child and always had a feeling that I had an invisible friend or something watching over me that I could turn to. I was too restless to enjoy being tied down to a desk at school, and teachers would tell my mother that I was "high strung," as though she didn't know. At a very early age my mother gave me a sage bit of advice, which I have followed to this very day. She would say, "Don't pray for anything. Just say 'Make me a better boy and show me the way.'"

Despite mother's advice I remember challenging God at an early age. During my childhood my mother, father, sister, and I attended the massive Travis Park Methodist Church in downtown San Antonio. We always sat in the balcony, and I remember that during the prayers I would ask God to lift me up and fly me out over the large open space so that people would look up and exclaim "Isn't that Walter Junior?"

My first memory of consciously questioning God happened when I was going on nine years of age. Just before the stock market crash of 1929, all the local Methodist Churches in San Antonio had a big missionary fundraising revival at the Municipal Auditorium. The Bishop gave a rousing talk, and the slots on the giant blackboard with squares for the names of contributors were soon filled. Two weeks later the crash hit, and the bank where the funds were deposited went under. I remember asking my mother "Wasn't that God's money?" Mother answered in the affirmative, and I responded, "Then why did God let it happen?"

I was nine years old when my father died, and I am told that I went around at his funeral with a smile on my face telling everyone, "Don't cry. Daddy's in heaven." When my grandmother died soon after my father I remember grabbing the Bible to take with me to her funeral.

At this time we had a Jewish neighbor who read Unity's Daily Word. To comfort mother she would pass on copies to her, and in turn mother read them to her nine-year-old son who took seriously everything his mother told him. Shortly thereafter we moved away and mother no longer had copies of the *Daily Word* to read to me, but looking back I feel the seeds of mysticism were planted then. Feeling that I needed male companionship, mother sent me to the YMCA summer camp the year after father died. When I would have attacks of homesickness I would go into the woods and sit in the outdoor chapel because I felt at peace there.

As the years went on I wasn't particularly religious or respectful of tradition and was quite capable of performing sacrilegious stunts. I remember that at age twelve my cousin and I slipped into the big Baptist church one mid-week day and saw that the baptismal pool was uncovered; so we stripped down and took a swim.

By the time I reached high school I was out to try everything. Thank goodness that drugs and mind-affecting substances were not popular in those days or I would doubtless have experimented. I do remember one embarrassing experience that took place when I was a sophomore in high school. One night my best friend, a Methodist bishop's son, and I were in a hotel in downtown San Antonio where a convention was taking place. A drunk offered me 50 cents for a paper hat I had found. We took the money and bought a 49 cent bottle of Muscatel wine. The bishop and his wife were away somewhere preaching. My friend and I drank the whole bottle of wine and were not only drunk but also sick to our stomachs when the bishop and his wife unexpectedly returned. When my mother came to pick me up the next morning my hangover was enough punishment and my mother made no further comment.

A profound turning point came when I was a senior in high school. Though I taught a Sunday school class of nine-year-olds—I wasn't drawn to organization and wasn't partial to any particular church denomination—I could imagine myself standing up before a congregation delivering an impassioned sermon, so I went to my minister to ask him if he thought I should be a preacher. He gave me the best advice of my life. He said, "Try not to be." I've spent eighty-five years trying not to be, but, despite the fact that I am not a member of any church or particular religion, in later years I have found myself somewhere behind a pulpit on many Sundays.

As time passed that minister's advice went deep into my feelings. By the time I went off to the University of Texas, I decided that I would let go of all formal religious beliefs until I had experienced something that proved itself and had real meaning for me. I felt it was more important for me to explore interpersonal relationships, to discover my sexual and sensual feelings, and as far as possible to separate myself from the traditions of the past.

After I left home and was on my own, I felt that the world was my oyster, that the sky was the limit, and that one way or the other I could manipulate life to get whatever I wanted. I was never shy or self-conscious in finding ways to play the game. Until my senior year at college when I was able to choose interesting subjects, I was no more than an average student, though I did participate in student activities and managed to get myself elected co-president of the student body at Trinity University in San Antonio.

I would go to church with my mother on visits at Easter and Christmas, but otherwise the Bible was a closed book for me, and study or search for spiritual meaning was not included in my agenda. Nevertheless, I always felt that there was a "something," and whether from superstition or not, I found myself repeating the Lord's Prayer and/or the 23 Psalm by rote every night before I went to sleep.

After graduating from Trinity, I went through mid-shipman school at Columbia in New York and served as a naval officer in World War II. The navy experience let me know that I didn't want to return to Texas and conform to the hypocrisies and rigid moral standards included in the mores of my youth; so on my discharge I went straight to New York where I could live in Greenwich Village and no one would point fingers at me for whatever life style I chose to live and, hopefully, there I would find my answers.

Shortly before my discharge from the navy my family church in Texas had sent me a little book of daily devotionals called *Abundant Living* by E. Stanley Jones, a prominent Methodist author who had lived in India for sixteen years. It lay unread in my quarters at the naval base at Guantanamo Bay, Cuba, where I was stationed at the end of the war. The day I was to leave I packed my bag and deposited the book in the trash along with other trivia. The plane on which I was to return to the States was delayed until the next morning, and not wanting to reappear at the officer's club where I had said my goodbyes, I looked for something to read and retrieved the little book of prayers from the trash, read a few of them, and somehow the little book ended up in the pocket of my raincoat on my return to the States. I found some comfort in it, and continued to read it as the days went by. I now realize that the Hindu hint of a subjective or mystical approach that had influenced the author's writings due to his stay in India had seeped into his messages, and it awakened something within me that I didn't recognize until I was exposed to Joel's mysticism and his explanation of there being a God within.

Nevertheless, at the end of the war I felt about as full of mental and psychological holes as a sieve. It was my nature to put a good face on things and trust that I would land on my feet; so part of me brushed aside the pitfalls of life in New York, while within I was actually loaded with anxiety. My nerves were so shot that I had blisters on my sweaty palms and my stomach would get upset at unlikely times. I remember one day—I was on my way for a job interview at ten in the morning—when nausea hit me and I found myself throwing up on the corner of 60th Avenue and 54th Street with passersby looking at me disgustedly as though I were a drunk.

Sometimes I would have to take things to pick me up and at other times things to calm me down. Something in me told me that it would be impossible for me to plug up all the holes in the sieve one by one through psychology, and that my only chance was to find some central meaning for life that would take care of all of my shortcomings at once. I desperately needed tracks to run on, though no one would suspect it because I always gave the impression that I was on top of things and that my life was a piece of cake.

God works in mysterious ways. One night I was bar-hopping in the Village and had consumed far too much to drink. Cutting through a dark alley on my way home, more than half-drunk, I was mugged. I was knocked down; the coat to my new suit was pulled off of my back, and along with it my wallet containing a considerable portion of my limited funds. I had enough change in my pocket to get me back to the room I had rented, a dinky room where one day my sleep was interrupted by a rat jumping onto my chest.

The morning after I was rolled in the Village I woke up with a black eye and a face puffy with bruises; so I couldn't continue looking for a job. Lying there helpless for a couple of days it was as though a dam opened up and all the muddy water ran out. In what I presently know was a kind of Epiphany, for the first time I was consciously aware of my inner spirit speaking to me, and this something said, "Study all the world's religions, because if you find truths that appear in all of them those truths can be trusted." And then it added, "Now you will be led to a teacher."

When those thoughts came into my head I thought I was losing my mind. What did it mean that I would be led to a teacher? In 1945 the world was a completely different place than it is today. To seek help, one either went to a psychologist or the church. Self-help studies were not yet standard fare. Gurus and spiritual guides were only popularized twenty years later when the Hippie generation came into being. The press and media shunned any reference whatsoever to there being an inner life. Few even dared talking about anything with spiritual implications under the guise that their spiritual life was a private matter; therefore, I felt uniquely alone and had no idea what it meant to be led to a teacher.

As for finding work, I had played the lead in the school play in my senior year at high school, a couple of plays in college, and had been an apprentice in a stock company in Connecticut one summer; so needing to find a job I decided that perhaps I could fake my way into the Broadway Theater as an actor. A few days after I recovered from my mugging, with a patch over my black eye, I went to audition for a part in a play and was eventually selected. The play was not successful and closed out of town, but that gave me the credentials I needed to try out for the juvenile lead in *The Mermaid Singing,* a new play by John van Druten, who, as I said, was the most successful playwright and director on Broadway at that time. The character was that of a young naval officer.

In order to appear self-confident at the reading and to remind them that I had just been an officer, at my audition I told them, "I started to wear my old uniform, but I thought that would be about as subtle as a lead pipe." It worked. I got the part, and that led to my introduction to Joel.

Joel S. Goldsmith, 1951

A young Joel Goldsmith.

John van Durten,
1952

Naval Officer,
Starcke, 1945

# The Message

*T*here is no place where the human story plays out and its spiritual implications begin; therefore, before this modern parable unfolds further and because it became the background music of my life, I want to quote a few passages from Joel's foundation book, *The Infinite Way*, for those who are not familiar with his writings. It took me years to understand the multi-layered first paragraphs that actually sum up Joel's entire message:

> *In the beginning was the Word, and the Word was with God, and the Word was God. . . . And the Word was made flesh.*
>
> *The Word was made flesh — but it still is the Word. By being made flesh it does not change its nature, character, or substance. Cause becomes visible as effect, but the essence or substance is still the Word, Spirit or Consciousness.*
>
> *In this wise, do we understand that there is not a spiritual universe and a material world, but rather that what appears as our world is the Word made flesh, Spirit made visible, or Consciousness expressed as idea.*
>
> *All the error that has existed down the ages is founded on the theory or belief of two worlds, one the heavenly kingdom, or spiritual life, and the other a material world or mortal existence, each separate from the other.*

In today's vernacular, when Joel said that by the word's becoming flesh does not change its nature, character, or substance, he was affirming what the founder of Quantum

Theory, Max Planck, stated early in the twentieth century—everything is consciousness appearing visibly as form or what the Christian Scientists call "substance."

Further along in *The Infinite Way*, Joel gave credence to material appearance by adding:

> *Let us begin with the understanding that our world is not an erroneous one, but rather that the universe in which we live is the realm of reality about which man entertains a false concept.*

Then he included a practical solution by what he called the first law of spiritual nature:

> *There is never a conflict with person or condition, but rather a false concept mentally entertained about person, thing, circumstance, or condition. Therefore, make the correction within yourself, rather than attempting to change anyone or anything in the without.*

The magnet that drew me to Joel's message was his pure mysticism. He repeatedly taught that:

> *There is not God and you, but that God is ever manifest as you, and this is the oneness which assures you of infinite good. God is the life, mind, body, and substance of individual being, therefore, nothing can be added to any individual, and true prayer is the constant recognition of this truth.*

"As" is the key word. It took a long time for me to relate that word to my own being, but then I realized that all that appears is God appearing "as" that; when I am in my right mind, God is appearing "as" my individual being. That truth eliminates my sense of duality and establishes me in Joel's absolute mysticism:

> *As we identify this God-being as the only reality of our individual being, we are able to comprehend ourselves as the fulfillment of being—all inclusive, immortal, and divine. The recognition of the divinity of our individual being, embracing and including the allness of God, is true prayer which is ever answered.*

Joel taught that man has the ability to experience his higher consciousness, which is God, and that in doing so all that he ordinarily went to God for would be accomplished. He also taught that knowing the nature of God was not enough.

We also have to know the nature of what he called "error," that which isn't God. To Joel, error, ignorance, or evils are lies claiming to be truths. By believing that a lie has power we give it that power and we suffer the consequences, when in fact we don't have to. If we know that error is a "nothingness" claiming to be a power, we can neutralize its effect. He claimed that if we do not just think of but rather experience God as the only power, then error will be "nothingized."

Encapsulating Joel's *Infinite Way* into these few condensed words is a gross oversimplification. His 35-plus books and thousands of hours of tape recorded lectures expound upon and extend the principles set forth here—and sometimes seem to contradict them!

CHAPTER TWO

# The Story Begins

One day after I got the part in the new van Druten play, which he also directed, John and I somehow got into a discussion about spiritual matters. He tried to explain to me the metaphysical approach to living, which was a foreign concept for me. Seeing that I was having trouble understanding, he said that he would write an article for me about what he believed. Two days later he gave it to me. I was surprised and impressed with the fact that as busy as he was he would take the time to write the article and that he cared enough about my interest to share his beliefs.

Although I thought there must be something profound in what John wrote, I wasn't familiar with metaphysics and his intellectual approach didn't register with me. The article was several thousand words long and I had a hard time even getting through it. As a sample, here are the two opening paragraphs of John's article which is titled, "What do I believe?"

*In the beginning is the truth. No matter where you start in religious belief or lack of it, your belief is your conception of truth. But today the eye of the microscope has shown us that the drop of water is a complete world of living, multiplying organisms instead of the simple clear liquid we perceive with our human senses.*

*The acceptance of the microscopic picture is an act of faith denying our limited senses. So, if this is the case, there must be truths about almost everything we humans see, touch, taste, and smell that are beyond our powers of comprehension. I can easily accept it that man is the son of truth in that one does have a greater knowledge of truth than any other living matter (certainly advanced over the bug that sees distance or depth as movement, etc.). But certainly we, too, are very limited and there are these other dimensions that man might someday develop that would completely change our whole view—and also set us free—for even in this limited state the more we know of truth the freer we become.*

*So, in the beginning is the truth. I accept the fact that my human senses limit my understanding of that truth and that truth that makes you free is what I mean by God, principle, Infinite invisible, or Brahman. But in accepting that fact, and living by it, I herald the extinction of my own ego—the representative of the senses—and that is where the whole struggle lies. As in trying to explain color to a blind man, trying to penetrate the ego and its by-product, the human intellect, with spiritual matter is a hopeless and almost lost cause. Therefore, to me the one great miracle is that the truth of spiritual light does*

*penetrate at all. The human intellect can lead
you up to the very end but it always deals with
human words or pictures, which are thereby
products of the human mind. For in truth, man
is not what his mind says and does even on the
human plane of conception.*

Frankly, after reading it, I didn't have a clue. I hadn't
yet studied Oriental philosophy with its subjective approach
to the nature of human existence, and logic wasn't my forte in
college. Seeing that I wanted to understand but couldn't quite
follow his metaphysical approach, van Druten then gave me
one of the letters that Joel was sending out to his patients at
that time and told me that it was written by a friend of his.
"This is a letter from a Christian Science practitioner," he said.
"With your Methodist background you won't understand it,
but read it and I will explain its meaning."

The next morning I started reading the letter and
bells went off, or I should say "exploded," in my head. It was
as though the letter was written just to me, and I had that
galvanizing experience people say happens to them when
they hear their God-given spiritual message for the first
time.

The letter was written in March of 1944. Though he
used the word "you," to address an impersonal reader, I took
it personally as though speaking only to me. When he said,
"Ye are the light of the world," I saw that he meant that I
was the light of the world, and if that is so there wasn't any
darkness in me at all and nothing could be added to me,
and that if I would accept this teaching I would "shine as the
noon-day sun." He said that because I am the light of the
world I "need not seek for light, health, riches, success, or
progress," but just for me to know "I am." That which I am
seeking I already am.

The letter went on to say that Jesus never said he would be resurrected, but he did say "I Am the resurrection." He never spoke of seeking the Truth, using Truth, applying the Truth but he said "I am the Truth." The letter told me to remember that Jesus not only said "I am the light" but also "Ye are the light of the world." "Greater works shall ye do." He promised that if I would accept the truth that I am the truth and abide steadfastly in this consciousness, all the petty trials and big problems of human existence would fade away.

He said to "sing within myself, morning, noon, and night, I am the life, the truth, the light," that I should let a song of joy and grateful recognition surge through my being and know that the divine being is my only being. "This being is all-inclusive life, love, substance, law, and reality."

He added that as I rested in this consciousness, I would no longer find it necessary to "overcome evil," struggle with difficulties, destroy ignorance, or battle human conditions, because this "I Am" is the universal Being, "your Christ-Self, your true identity, the only one you have."

And sing I did! When I finished reading the letter the weight of the world seemed to lift off my shoulders. I couldn't wait to tell van Druten that this had awakened something in me that I felt I had always known subconsciously but had never heard crystallized in words before. When I saw him the next day, instead of waiting for his explanation, I burst forth with youthful zeal and enthusiasm as though I had singularly understood what was in the letter. I felt I had discovered a spiritual gold mine and proceeded to flood John with questions about Joel and his teaching.

In recounting his experiences with Joel, John told me about an incident that happened at the Boston tryout of his play, *I Remember Mama*. As divine providence would have it, Joel happened to be in town at that time and John had given him a 3rd-row aisle seat for the opening. The production depended on a complicated change of sets. There was a small turntable on each side of the stage that revolved for different vignettes and a large turntable in the center for major set changes. Everything had to work in concert and exactly on time.

Just before the curtain was scheduled to go up John came down and asked Joel to come with him. At the back of the theater John told Joel that the turntables were stuck and weren't working so they couldn't start the play. Joel asked where he could go and be alone for a moment and was shown into the men's lounge. In just a few minutes, "lo! and behold!" the turntables began to move and the show opened flawlessly.

Sensing my avid interest in Joel's teaching, John suggested that I write to him in Hollywood, where Joel was living at that time. I took his suggestion, and that began a personal relationship that lasted until Joel's death eighteen years later.

I couldn't afford to keep my rented room for the weeks we were on the road with *The Mermaids Singing* so I let it go. When we returned to New York I looked for another room close to the theater. During and shortly after the war most hotels limited stays to five days; however, there was a shabby little hotel in the theater district where I could rent a room on a permanent basis. When I inquired I found that there was another young actor who needed a roommate to share the rent. I met him. He was about my age and seemed nice enough; so I accepted.

After the play opened, John returned to his ranch in California and I had no one that I could talk to or lean on to help me through the first challenging experience I encountered that tested my newfound beliefs. The resilience of youth, coupled with the letters and writings I was receiving from Joel, got me through what could have been a traumatic setback.

The room I had rented in the sleazy hotel was depressing, to say the least. It had a single window that opened onto a dark court. Even though it was mid-winter and the window was wide open, no fresh air would come in and the pipes in the wall kept the room hot as a sauna all the time. The overhead light in the room was seldom turned on because I wouldn't get home after my performance until one or two in the morning and my roommate would be asleep. In the morning he would leave early looking for work. Not wanting to disturb each other, the bedroom remained dark almost all the time and we individually seemed to spend most of our waking time there in the bathroom. On other days I would leave after noon to either play a matinee or tend to other business and he would be asleep on my return.

Finally there were a couple of days when I would wake up and see that my roommate was in his bed apparently asleep; so not to disturb him I dressed in the bathroom and left. However, when I came home one afternoon to get ready to go to the theater I was stopped at the desk. A maid had come into the room for the weekly change of the towels and sheets and found that my roommate had taken sleeping pills. I had been living with a dead body for a couple of days and didn't know it. To top it off, I had to pay his half of the bill in order to retrieve my things and move to another hotel. I got through it, superstitiously or not, by repeating a passage from Joel's letter: "Don't judge by appearances. If you accept this teaching you will shine as the noon-day sun in which there is no darkness at all." I clung to his teaching that the "I Am" of me would take care of all my needs.

Unfortunately, the mermaid stopped singing after

a few months and the play was John's first failure in years; so once more I hit the pavement looking for work. As there was no one I knew in New York with whom I could discuss my newfound passionate interest in spiritual matters, I began to read anything and everything I could find of a mystical nature. I read Joel's letters over and over, along with Emerson, the Unity writings of the Fillmores, and Ernest Holmes's *Science of Mind*. Even though I hadn't been a particularly good student during my school years and had difficulty reading complicated prose, I found I was able to read the most esoteric spiritual or metaphysical texts with avid interest and comprehension. My search for answers became the major and continuing lifetime motivation for my life from then on.

Before long I got another leading part in a five-character Broadway show called *This Too Shall Pass* that opened in the spring to mixed notices. Believing that the play would inevitably live up to its title and pass on before the summer was over, I began to look for another job. All the young actors were trying out for the lead opposite the English actress, Dame Mae Whitty, for a summer stock tour of the play *Night Must Fall*, which had brought her to America and ultimately Hollywood fame. I joined the group.

The finals came down to a young actor named Marlon Brando and me. I got the part! That was not because I was a better actor but because Brando was difficult to understand or cope with even then. The producer thought that as I was a polite, respectful young man, I would be a better companion for the eighty-two year old actress during the tour.

Once on tour I was amazed to find out that Dame Mae, who lived in Hollywood, was also a client of Joel's. When she learned of my interest in him she talked about him throughout the summer. As Joel didn't have that many followers in Hollywood at that time I felt my being with Dame Mae was another example of divine synchronicity; so I decided to go out to California to meet him at the end of the summer.

## *Meeting Joel*

*W*hen I arrived in Los Angeles, van Druten met me at the airport and took me to his apartment in the Chateau Marmont, the most fashionable apartment building in Hollywood. That afternoon he told me that Joel was writing a book and that van Druten had been asked to write the introduction; so I literally read the introduction to *The Infinite Way*, Joel's first book, before he read it.

The following morning I went for the prearranged appointment with Joel at his office on Hollywood Boulevard across the street from Grumman's Chinese Theater. I got off the elevator in anticipation and stood in front of the office door emblazoned with the words "Joel S. Goldsmith, C.S." (Christian Science). When I read that inscription I felt my saintly grandfather turn over in his grave. He was a doctor, my father was a doctor, and my uncle was a doctor, and I had heard them being appalled at Christian Scientists who allowed their children to suffer and die because they would not seek medical help. I felt as though I were about to enter a house of spiritual prostitution.

I knocked on the door expecting my mentally pre-packaged image of a tall, benign, fatherly figure wearing the look of a patient, loving, other-worldly master to appear. The door opened and my eyes dropped down to the five-foot-four, curly-haired, smiling, round-faced, portly little Jewish man wearing a string tie and a bright plaid sports coat, with a humorous twinkle in his eye.

The office was rather sterile and without any decoration or ambiance that would encourage spiritual exaltation or intimate discussion. There were no religious symbols or the smell of incense. I do remember that on his desk was a bud vase with a single red rose, a Bible, and a copy of *Science and Health*. Later, I saw that Joel always had a fresh flower at his meditation spot. I can't remember what we talked about at this first meeting, because I was probably trying harder to impress Joel than I was in listening to what he had to say. Nevertheless, I do remember feeling an easy, gentle power and authority emanate from his presence.

The next day was the weekend, and Joel, Nadea, John, and I drove down to John's ranch in the desert. The ranch house was in the center of a forest of date palms in lines with rows of corn growing between the trees. The charming Spanish style adobe home was built around a patio next to a football-field-sized cemented cistern that served as his swimming pool. The flagstone terrace with the diving board at the deep end of the pool was shaded by towering cottonwood trees. We were shown to our rooms where we put on our bathing suits for a swim. I was speedy and at poolside before the rest came out.

A few minutes later, Joel appeared in baggy swimming trunks and a sleeveless t-shirt with shiny white stuff all over his face, making him look like a circus clown. Half amused and half shocked, I asked what he had on his face. Without any sense of embarrassment or chagrin he said, "I sunburn." I thought, "What's this! Christian Science practitioners sunburn!" Actually, by the time he moved to Hawaii he must have healed himself because he swam in the ocean daily and never sunburned again as far as I know.

The weekend was full of laughter, small talk, and luxury. We were waited on at every turn by John's cook and butler. These few days with Joel were the beginning of my 18-year period of personal contact with him. Whenever we were in the same place—be it Hollywood, Hawaii, London, or New York—we saw each other almost every day. When I wasn't in his presence, I wrote him letters at least once a week for years to come, and he always answered them promptly.

After being exposed firsthand to Joel's teaching, my whole life took on a new meaning. Death and resurrection do not happen once in a lifetime, but many times over. Every time we have a shift in consciousness, no matter how small, we become slightly different people. We may look the same, and for the time being the conditions in our lives may appear to be similar to what they were before, but like proceeding beyond a fork in a road, as time goes on we get further and further away from the life and conditions we lived in before.

Joel treated everyone with the same friendly but detached manner, and I was no exception. Nevertheless, I felt that he had a secret, an inner presence that somehow gave him a direct line to the source of truth. It was as though he were simultaneously in tune with a whole different dimension than we ordinary humans. I knew that I had to find out what that mysterious something was. I was far more interested in spending time with him than anyone else and couldn't wait to be in his presence again.

I would have considered moving to Hollywood except that I felt that New York City was my monastery. I knew that in the past people thought that the way to evolve spiritually was for one to leave the world, enter a monastery, cut one's self off from all human attachments, give up all earthly possessions, and forcibly discipline one's ego out of existence. I instinctively felt that running away from the shadow side of life and materialistic temptations was only a temporary solution and not the answer for me. I felt that if I could find the answer in New York, the materialistic capital of the world, I could be at peace anywhere. That began a kind of love-hate relationship with New York City. It was my testing ground, and I knew that until I was as happy to be there as anywhere I couldn't leave.

# Swami Prabhavananda and the Vedanta Monastery

There is one more character in this drama, a feature player who held a prominent place in John's and my spiritual evolution and was highly respectful of Joel's work—Swami Prabhavananda.

While I was in California, John took me to the Vedanta monastery in Trabuco Canyon above Laguna Beach on the edge of a national forest where Swami Prabhavananda was in residence when he was not at their temple in Hollywood or convent in Santa Barbara. It was at the monastery that I eventually spent time with Aldous Huxley, Christopher Isherwood, Gerald Heard, and other frequent visitors who were at the forefront of combining Western and Eastern philosophy.

The monastery was, and is, a remarkable place with rambling brick buildings built around patios with small cell-like private rooms for the monks, a separate cottage for visitors, a large communal dining room, and a beamed ceiling lodge room with a fireplace where Swami would sit cross-legged in a big overstuffed chair after dinner, surrounded by the monks and visitors, discussing the Upanishads and other Hindu scriptures.

The heart of the monastery was a round windowless sanctuary adjoining the residential buildings where we would sit on carpeted semicircular tiers before the altar with its large gilt-framed picture of the almost naked Hindu saint, Ramakrishna, the founder of the order, smiling down on us with a haunting, faraway look of divine love. The swami, clothed in his ocher robe, would sit before the altar with its countless burning pots of ghee, flower garlands, offerings of food, and the glittering polished brass bell and other articles of their ceremonies.

I will always be eternally grateful for my initial visit to the monastery because it was there that I had my first meditation experience. Still highly keyed and desperately needing to find ways to calm down without having to use store-bought tranquilizers, I took to meditation in a big way. It was more than an exercise. Meditation became a necessity. Though I would join the monks when they meditated for an hour before breakfast, lunch, and dinner, when the hour was over they had to practically drag me out of the sanctuary.

In a way, on that first visit to the monastery, I felt that I was breathing air for the first time—both spiritual and artistic air. I felt inspired and completely unthreatened and un-judged by the gentle loving spirit that filled the monastery. The sound of good-humored laughter was music to the soul. The smell of fresh cut flowers and incense permeated the air, and the senses-titillating taste and aroma of the different curries accompanied by lime pickles and mango chutney were a treat at every meal. Everything was in the best of simple taste. I had never experienced anything so humanly self-nurturing before. Something in me wanted to stay forever in that loving ambiance; however, I knew that escaping from the world was not my answer.

Swami Prabhavananda was wonderful to me. He never demanded that I become initiated into the order and yet he let me join in with the monks during his teaching periods and meditations. On one memorable occasion at the temple in Hollywood he invited me, along with a dozen others, to lunch with him and Paramhansa Yogananda, who established the Self-Realization Fellowship and whose *Autobiography of a Yogi* has become a classic. The affection and bond between those two oriental masters was palatable and inspiring.

I greatly appreciate what I learned through Swami Prabhavananda over the many years in which I would visit the monastery, but also what I recieved from him about the beauty of the spiritual subtleties inherent in the Vedanta message, and much more through the caring, loving, and compassionate spirit expressed by the man himself. As a man, he showed me what we human beings are personally capable of.

Joel had a great respect for Swami, and though he taught that once one finds one's teacher one should stop shopping around, Joel none-the-less approved of my visiting the monastery, and encouraged my studying all religions and the different mystical approaches.

Joel and Emma in Hawaii.

Walter in *The Druids Circle*, 1947, with Susan Douglas

John van Durten, 1949.

58

CHAPTER THREE

# The Transition Years

*I*t wasn't until I read Lorraine Sinkler's *The Spiritual Journey of Joel S. Goldsmith,* published in 1973, that I realized the divine synchronicity that took place in Joel's and my life at the time of our first meeting in 1946. In her book, Lorraine quoted a letter Joel had written to her which said, "In 1946, a year after I was told that would be my year of transition…in July the spiritual experience of initiation began and lasted for two months."

It was during those two months that I met Joel personally and had my initiation into his consciousness. At that time he was completing *The Infinite Way* and beginning his individual teaching, and I was actually his first Infinite Way student. Everyone who had come to him previously had come through Christian Science, but I had no metaphysical background at all, and all of my future training was fashioned by being introduced to his unique interpretation of the Christ message.

On returning from that first visit to California and my initiation to a new level of consciousness, my life began to change. The first thing I did in the morning was to meditate. Joel had told me that there was nothing more important than setting aside enough time each morning for it. I didn't have to discipline myself to make space for that meditation time. I relished it, and I found that my morning meditations soon became a habitual necessity. That single practice changed my daily life.

I soon began to experience what seemed like adverse fallout from my commitment to meditate each morning. I lost many of my friends. Theater people ordinarily stay up until the wee small hours, partly because after a performance they need time to come back down to earth and let the tension subside, often getting home to bed at two or three in the morning. In order to get up early enough to meditate before going out to look for work, I would cut out on my friends just as they were getting started and I would say, "Sorry fellows. I have to leave now." It wasn't long before I was dropped from the group.

Joel had told me that one of the main reasons for me to meditate was that through reaching the inner silence I would hear the still small voice and receive its intuitive guidance. Oddly enough, when I began to meditate daily something I hadn't expected took place. I had always had a chronic sinus condition and spent a lot of my time in the winter months with a handkerchief at my nose. Up until one of these meditations, I had an all-American-boy habit of drinking a pint of milk before going to bed at night. At that time it wasn't well known that milk causes mucus. Despite its not seeming logical, my meditation told me to break the habit and stop drinking milk. I did so, and my sinus problem promptly cleared up, never to return.

Though I asked for and received help from Joel in terms of my emotional or psychological problems, I never asked him for material benefits. In all the years of my relationship with Joel, I never got a so-called "spiritual healing" of a physical problem from him—but when my consciousness began to absorb the principles of his teaching, I stopped getting sick and didn't need physical healings. I never asked Joel to help increase my income, but by filling my consciousness with the Infinite Way principles, success in the theater came and so did abundance.

Because of our mutual attraction to Joel's teaching, my relationship with John van Druten deepened, and when he was in New York I would also see him almost every day. While Joel satisfied my hunger for spiritual meaning in an impersonal way, my appetite for the arts, travel, fine cuisine, and human relationship was satisfied personally by John. I was eager to learn and was a human sponge, soaking it all up. On the other hand, John appreciated sharing his wealth of literate knowledge, his appreciation of the arts, and his refined culture with me without feeling that what he had to offer was being wasted.

# The Sierra Bonita Years

*T*he Infinite Way was published early in 1947. Having sent in his resignation to Christian Science headquarters, Joel gave up his office and moved into his home on Sierra Bonita, a block off of Sunset Boulevard in the heart of Hollywood. The house was a typical 1920s single storied, California shingle and wood, two-bedroom cottage with a couple of palm trees in the front yard. As you entered, the living room was off to the right and on the left Joel had put a desk in what was intended to be the dining room and made it into his office.

That year marked another major change for Joel. After leaving the organization he thought he would simply have a healing practice and perhaps do a bit of teaching. He had no idea how his work would expand and what a powerfully effective speaker he would become. He began by having a few people come to his home once a week for instruction. That soon became two nights a week and ultimately every night. In no time his home could not hold all those who came for group instruction, so he rented a meeting hall. His reputation grew to the point that he was asked to go to San Francisco and give some talks in a metaphysical book store on the second floor of a building that is a block from the Saint Francis Hotel.

On Joel's first talk at the book store in San Francisco, before a group of people unacquainted with his work, he panicked, got cold feet, and wanted to back out. Nadea, his wife, had to practically push him onto the platform. Once Joel began to speak, however, the Spirit took over, and he never had the problem to that extent again.

Joel's lectures at the book store were taken down in shorthand and made into mimeographed manuscripts. Initially they were called *The First, Second,* and *Third San Francisco Lectures* but were later edited and made into the books: *Metaphysical Notes, The Master Speaks, Consciousness Unfolding,* and *God, the Substance of All Form.*

Joel's old fear of being a spiritual vagabond, unable to find his place, was now being replaced by his long hoped-for belief that he had a special calling and his self-confidence grew. Joel spoke in a number of Unity churches during that year and his name began to spread throughout the New Thought movement. As it did, a new metaphysical star was being born.

# My Second Visit

While Joel's public work was expanding, my acting career took off. I played leads on television for Studio

One and Philco Playhouse—the two hour-long weekly hit dramas—played in summer stock, and signed to play a leading part in a November Broadway production of *The Druid's Circle* at the Morosco Theater.

The play flopped and closed at the end of the month. Although I didn't personally get any bad notices, when a play fails everything goes down the drain with it. Frustrated with the turn my career had taken, having no appetite to hit the pavement once more, and anxious to spend more time with Joel and John, I sublet my apartment and went to California to study with Joel.

At my first appointment with Joel in his house on Sierra Bonita I sat across the desk from him in a distraught and anxious frame of mind. He asked me why I had left New York and I told him that apart from wanting to see him I didn't really know. I was at a loss and almost in tears as he questioned me about what I planned to do. Joel closed his eyes and after a minute of silence he turned to me, and with unquestionable authority said, "When you get up in the morning don't meditate. Just turn your concerns over to God and me, and go about your life." I did just what he ordered. I got up each morning and said, "OK God, it is up to you and Joel."

On the second day I ran into a director on the street that I had worked for in New York. He asked me why I was in Hollywood and I told him that I didn't know. He informed me that he was the program director for television station KLRN, the only commercial station operating in Los Angeles at that time; the cable connecting New York and California was only completed early the next year, making CBS and NBC available on the coast. My director friend asked me if I would like to be a television director. Of course, I jumped at the opportunity and took the job, feeling in my heart that it was the direct result of Joel's intercession.

During the several months that I had that job, I stayed in John's spare bedroom at the Chateau Marmont and would visit Joel regularly. On some of my days off I would go to the Vedanta monastery to sit with Swami and the monks. For recreation, I would go to the beach and play volleyball.

During this time I would read *The Infinite Way* over and over every day trying to make sense out of what was happening in my life. A particular passage remains in my memory:

> *While thought is on the picture before us—"this world"—we are engaged in the constant effort to improve or change it. As soon as we lift our vision—take our thought off what we shall eat and drink and wear—we begin to behold spiritual reality which appears to us as improved beliefs, but which really is more—appearing as reality. This more-appearing reality brings with it joys untold here and now, pleasures beyond our wildest imagination, and the love of all with whom we come in contact, even the love of those who do not know the source of the new life we have discovered.*

One day, after I had a number of sessions with Joel, he asked me to join him in meditation. Contrary to some practitioners, he did not meditate one-on-one with those who came to him until he felt that they were ready for the experience. That first meditation had quite an impact on me. Joel sat behind his desk and on the other side I faced him at a bit of an angle. He closed his eyes, knitted his brow, and, with intense concentration, appeared to be listening to an inner voice. Shortly after we began to meditate the side of my face turned toward Joel became hot, as though I was sitting next to a furnace, and I felt a magnetic pull as though I was literally being drawn out of myself. I knew that something powerful was happening to me and I was more in awe of Joel than ever before. In those days I said very little, never questioned him on anything, and didn't comment about what I had experienced.

On one of those early sessions with Joel he completely deflated me. I thought it was obvious that I was totally and passionately dedicated to following his teaching, so I felt hurt and rejected when in an off-handed way he said, "You'll do all right if you stick with it." If I stick with it! I felt that with his great inner wisdom he should have known how deeply committed I was, and that there was no way that I could possibly turn away. When you least expected it, Joel could shake you up with a caustic comment.

The night after Joel's challenge I tried unsuccessfully to pray in order to regain my confidence. In exasperation I opened my copy of *The Infinite Way* at random and got a message re-confirming my sense of who I was:

> *I AM. God is the mind and the life of the individual. There is but one universal "I" whether it is being announced by Jesus Christ or John Smith. "I am the way, the truth, and the life." God is the only I, and "We are the place where God becomes visible. The nature of prayer is not an appeal to God but rather an actual experience of God."*

During this time in California a great deal of what Joel was teaching me began to sink in and I began to change the goals I had set for myself. Material success became less important to me and meditation grew from a chore to the highlight of my day. Each morning before getting out of bed I would say to myself before I started my day:

*This is the day the Lord hath made. I rejoice in it. The ground on which I stand is holy ground. I am heir and joint heir with Christ to all the heavenly riches. There is one power, one cause, and I am that. Thank you father. It is done.*

After a few months of my studying with Joel and working at the television station, the person who had sublet my apartment in New York moved out. My inner guidance then told me it was time for me to go back to my monastery and put into practice what Joel had taught me; so I returned to New York. On my return I remained in constant contact with Joel through our correspondence.

One letter written on January 29, 1948 shortly after my return to New york particularly pleased me. He began it by saying, "Well, dear friend, you have certainly come a long way since a year ago," and that a letter of mine he had just received was as "heartening a message" as he would hope to read. He went on to say that only when we think about obtaining objects that we desire do we miss the mark, and reported on an article he had read stating that the most powerful men in America who controlled more wealth than the government itself all ended up in mental institutions, suicide, or broke because they had learned everything except how to live.

More often Joel's messages to me were shorter and more cryptic than those he wrote to John. Mixed with compassion, they often showed the Old Testament demanding authoritarian side of Joel that easily intimidated me and his other close students. On September 14, 1950 he wrote, "I expect you to know that even before your call reaches me-the answer is where you are." He added that he expected me to know the answer and receive help before he got my call.

In response to some of my bellyaching, Joel wrote an even more caustic one-line letter on March 12, 1952, saying "you tried hard to convince me that you accept appearances for reality," but that I should not fall for that. Joel's unerring instinctive guidance seemed infallible. When I tried to get him to accept my limitations, he punctured my balloon, but more importantly, when I felt I was bogging down an encouraging letter would arrive reminding me of who I really was. My mail box became the treasure chest that I eagerly opened daily in anticipation.

CHAPTER FOUR

# The Theater Years

*D*uring the next two years both van Druten and I were in constant contact with Joel and we both discussed our frustrations and professional needs with him. At dinner one night on one of his frequent trips to New York, John complained that he was miserable because he wanted to write another play but couldn't come up with an idea that appealed to him. More by listening than thinking I heard myself suggest an idea: "Why not write a play about a modern-day witch living in New York. It could include all kinds of metaphysical principles. After all, when we humanly manipulate others or tip a head waiter in order get a table in a crowded restaurant, that, too, is modern witchcraft."

John leaped at the idea, conceiving of it first as a serious play, but I felt the metaphysical principles would be better disguised as a comedy. Out of that discussion came the Broadway play *Bell, Book and Candle* starring Rex Harrison and Lilly Palmer, and ultimately the movie version starring Jimmy Stewart, Kim Novak, and Jack Lemmon. Though few people caught the underlying significance of the play, it was an enormous success.

When he got ready to write the play, John asked me to come to his ranch and work on it with him. His Spanish-style home on the ranch had a wing on either side of a patio connected to the main house by a covered walkway. His office and bedroom were in one wing, and the guest wing opposite included a bedroom, bath, and sitting room where I spent hours in meditation every morning on my visits.

Often I didn't see John until noon because he rose early, made himself a cup of tea in his office, and began writing. Nevertheless, when I was there to help write a play I had to stay alert and ready to instantly drop whatever I was doing and focus my attention on his work. At any minute John might call me to come to his office to bounce an idea off me or he might ask me to help solve a script problem.

One day, during the writing of *Bell, Book and Candle,* John called me over to see if I had an answer for a problem. I didn't, and when we couldn't think of an answer to the blockage we decided to meditate. Remembering Joel's often-repeated principle of letting go and letting God, we surrendered our personal effort and arrived at the place where we heard, "I of my own self can do nothing." Boom! Immediately the solution appeared.

Consequently, the next day when another problem loomed we thought, "That's simple. All we have to do is think 'I of my own self can do nothing. I of my own self can do nothing,'" and nothing was exactly what we received. Alarmed, we went back into meditation, only this time we didn't take it lightly and really meant it. When we really let go, once more the answer to our problem came to light. Joel always taught that it was not the thinking of thoughts that made things happen but rather that one had to experience the consciousness of the thought in order to produce results.

At the road tryout of *Bell, Book and Candle* in Boston, the critics said that the play fell to pieces in the second act, and as a result we received mixed notices, some positive and others negative. In a suite at the Ritz Carlton Hotel, John, Irene Selznick (who produced the play), and I tossed things around long into the night. Finally, when I got quiet enough to listen to my intuition, I remembered Joel saying that once we got our egos out of the way we had access to omniscience or all-knowingness. And then I "heard" what the problem was.

At the end of the first act, Gillian, the leading lady, had bewitched a man she fancied into dropping his engagement with another woman and proposing to her. The second act had a lot of humorous and fascinating talk between Gillian and her family of witches, but there wasn't any plot or story line adding tension until the end of the act at which time the man she had bewitched finally saw that she was a witch and walked out on her. I pointed the problem out and John found a quick solution. He simply had Gillian's brother, played by Jack Lemmon in the picture, come in early in the act, at which time she told him of her impending marriage. Her brother said he didn't want her to marry, so he promised to witch her before the day was out and she's forget all about the marriage. That's all. We then went right on with the script just as it was, but with that threat hanging over the plot the audience attention held and the play opened in New York to smash hit reviews.

My spiritually-guided intuition gave John further confidence in my abilities. After the play's success, when the play was published, in the printed edition he included a dedication to me that said "With thanks for your help and for living through it from the beginning." My work on *Bell,*

*Book and Candle* led John to make me his assistant when he directed the original Broadway production of Rodgers and Hammerstein's *The King and I* later that year.

During the rehearsals for *The King and I*, something happened that represents what the relationship between an actor and his director or a spiritual leader and his student should be. John was pushing Yul Brynner to get him to respond physically, emotionally, and domineeringly in order to create chemistry between the King and Anna. Yul stopped up stage and in a rather rough tone said, "John!", and started coming down to the footlights. John reached over to me and said, "Oh dear, what have I done now?" Yul got to the foots and said, "John, you are my mirror. Give me my performance." Smart actor, John did, and Yul lived his life on it. I equate that statement with Joel's mission in my life. I felt that Joel was holding up a mirror to show me my true identity.

That realization brought to mind another quote from *The Infinite Way:*

> *Bringing health and harmony into our experience is not, then, getting rid of, or even changing, a mortal material universe, but rather by correcting the finite concept of our existence...Spiritual sense does not remove us from our normal surroundings, nor does it deprive us of the love and companionship so necessary to a full life. It merely places it on a higher level where it is no longer at the mercy of chance, change, or loss, and where the spiritual value of the so-called human scene is made manifest.*

# The Monastic Years

During the time when John and I started working on *Bell, Book and Candle* and its final production over a year later, I paid Joel another visit and continued my daily study. Though I thought I was making progress I felt that I was stuck in the middle. On the one hand I was still caught up in competitive, ambitious goals, doing whatever it took to become successful, and I still had the sexual and materialistic appetites of a lively 28-year-old. On the other hand, I wanted to surrender to the spiritual laws that Joel was teaching me, such as being a beholder of life rather than a manipulator of it and to trust the process.

Instead of tracking down every possible lead, I tried to let Spirit provide my opportunities for jobs. As a result, I didn't get any work apart from a few low-paying television appearances. My bank account went down and down. The more I meditated and the harder I tried to make the principles work, the worse it got.

Finally, I wrote Joel and asked him what was going on. He wrote me back and said, "Who do you think you are. Why don't you go work for a living?" I was stunned and responded, "You said that if there was one theater in the world, and I had the consciousness of theater, I would be at work in it." He wrote me back a worse letter, which I can't quote because I threw it away in disgust. Despite my being so beholden to Joel in the past, I covered up my feeling of rejection by thinking, "Joel doesn't understand his own teaching. I'll read the writings that come through him, but I'm not going to have any more to do with him as a person."

Now that I was turning to that which I had within myself and was no longer looking for Joel to be a witch doctor magically manifesting a job for me, I got one. The following week I auditioned for a play by Sidney Kingsley called *Detective Story*, which ran on Broadway for two years and was made into a successful movie starring Kirk Douglas. I got a leading part in the road company and was soon transferred to the Broadway cast. When we opened on the road in Detroit, Michigan another of those unexplainable divine synchronicities took place. It was the only week that Joel was ever in Detroit during his spiritual career. As I had come to realize that Joel's pushing me had caused me to turn to that which I had within myself, and as Joel didn't know I wasn't going to talk to him any more, I called him up. He invited me to come see him at his hotel near the theater in downtown Detroit.

When I went to Joel's suite I talked up to him more personally than I ever had before. Previously, I was so in awe of him that I hardly spoke, but this time I said, "Joel, if you tell me that sin, sickness, poverty, and such are not powers at some spiritual level, all right, but for me they are powers." He got a rather prissy look on his face, smiled, and answered, "Precisely, and if you want to stay a human being under those laws, help yourself, but you don't have to." Wow! I saw that it was up to me. I could choose to live by material law or by spiritual freedom.

We went on talking for some time and finally Joel said, "Let's meditate." Joel sat in a chair to my right and put his brown *Thompson Chain-Reference Bible* in his lap. We closed our eyes and began to meditate. Once more I felt a strong pull of energy coming from Joel. After a while I experienced a kind of shock go up my spine through my body—from my tailbone up to the top of my head. Though I didn't realize what was happening at the time, I suspect that what took place was what Hindus would say was the opening of my

Kundalini. When that happens the energy goes up from the bottom chakra through to the top one, similar to the seven energy centers Edgar Cayce talked of, or the nervous centers neurologists report.

When I had that experience with Joel, I wasn't particularly impressed at that moment, because I thought that the shock that went through me was just a chill or some physical quirk. We finished and I went back to my hotel to prepare for the play's evening performance. I decided to meditate once more, and when I did, the same physical experience took place as it had with Joel. I felt this energy rise from my lower spine up to the top of my head. I knew then that something really important had happened to me.

Joel would be the first person to say that one does not have to have a guru or another person to light their fire as some religions teach, but that the invisible Christ could make it happen without human intercession. Nevertheless, it did happen to me through this contact with Joel. That is also why I am eternally grateful to him or the Christ consciousness in him. The ability to repeat that experience of the presence within became the motivation of my life, and remains the same today.

After that extraordinary experience with Joel I went out and bought a brown *Thompson's Chain-Reference Bible* like Joel's, and to this day I meditate with my hand on it as Joel did. I do it not out of superstition but rather to be conscious of the presence of the Word and to be omnipresent with the life-affirming truths contained in the Scriptures.

After Detroit we played Chicago, and Joel asked me to give two talks at the Metaphysical Library, which is no longer in existence. I was surprised that Joel thought I was up to it; those talks were the first time I had ever attempted to share my beliefs with others.

Instead of trusting the spirit to tell me what to say, I made an outline that incorporated some of Joel's teachings that were important to me. The list included *The Infinite Way* interpretations of soul, life, spirit, supply, and error. I went on to say that we cannot know man until we know God, how we are branches of a spiritual tree, that our real existence is Spirit, sin is the belief in an existence apart from God, mortality is a myth, and I repeated a number of Scriptures.

Before I left Chicago I met with a follow-up group in the home of Laura Perkinpine, who later became one of Joel's inner circle. Lorraine Sinkler, who was an elementary school teacher in Chicago at that time, also came to the talks. That group became the first regularly-meeting group to study *The Infinite Way*, and after Laura Perkinpine left the area, Lorraine carried on.

When I was sent back to New York, I settled into the run of *Detective Story* on Broadway and returned to my old way of life. Then something happened that let me know the experience I had in meditation with Joel in Detroit had changed everything. At twenty-eight years of age I was hardly impotent, yet when I attempted a couple of casual sexual escapades I found that I could no longer perform as I had in the past. When I meditated on what was happening to me it became clear that making my spiritual contact in meditation every morning and night had become the most important thing in my life. I knew then that I had to eliminate anything that stood in the way; therefore, the time had come for me to deliberately and completely free myself of any external influences or appetites, anything that might possibly keep me from my making contact with the Spirit within.

I didn't give those things up for moral reasons, but rather because I wanted to leave no stone unturned that might keep me from experiencing the presence of God. I had completely accepted the implication in Joel's teaching that we could absolutely and totally impersonalize ourselves and become completely free of physical laws; I put my whole self into living it as absolutely as he said it could be done.

It was then that I ran headlong into the impossibility of absolutes. Joel's absolute teaching gave me nowhere to hide! I found that I couldn't blame anyone, my government, or anything else for my problems because my life was solely an out-picturing of my own consciousness; therefore, there was no such thing as an accident in my life. I might complain about my problems to others, but when I got home and had to face myself I had to admit that the cause of my problems was in my consciousness, and if I wanted to change anything I had to change my consciousness. That eventually led to what I call my monastic years.

During the next two years I attempted to absolutely overcome all human attachments or appetites whatsoever. For instance, if I had one or two martinis at dinner I could still meditate before going to bed, but I found that if I had the third martini there would be too much alcohol in my system for me to be able to make contact. The very time when I needed to meditate most would be the time I would take the third drink; so I eventually stopped all drinking, including wine. As far as sex was concerned, it wasn't a matter of the effect sex had on me physically, but rather how contemplating it and putting energy into expectations affected my consciousness and made my meditations more difficult; so, there too, out!

Smoking was the most difficult thing for me to give up. I didn't smoke more than a few cigarettes a day, but I believed that I had to have a smoke before I went to sleep, or to calm me down after I came off stage. I tried to stop smoking by sheer willpower and failed. Sometimes I would throw my cigarettes away, but when bedtime came I couldn't go to sleep and had to go out and buy another pack.

Once more, Joel played a part in my attempt to be absolute. On one of my trips to visit him I mentioned my difficulty in stopping smoking. That night after seeing Joel I returned to my hotel and once in bed I reached out for a cigarette. My salvia glands were working and I was ready. When I started to light the cigarette I heard my inner voice say, "It's twelve o'clock here in Hawaii. That means it is five in the morning in New York. How does that cigarette know what time it is?" I saw that the cigarette's power was in my mind and not in the cigarette. I put it down and went to sleep. The next day I bought some licorice to help me and never smoked again.

Joel knew that I was trying hard to transform my life, but I seldom talked to him about it in specific terms, and he never suggested that I go to the extreme that I did. In fact, when I told him about being tempted by the beauties on the beach in Hawaii or what I considered to be my other potentially sinful desires, he brushed them aside and said, "Don't worry about it. Do your spiritual work and when they have served their purpose they will go away. You just keep your eye on your spiritual progress and everything will take care of itself."

By the time I became a producer at age thirty, I was almost completely abstinent of any overt physical appetites. My monastic period came into full bloom and lasted for seven years, further isolating me from my peer-group contemporaries in the theater. Joel and John, who were both over 20 years older than I, knew that my heart was intent on achieving spiritual enlightenment in any way that I could, if not to the extent I was pushing myself, and their understanding and encouragement were my support.

    In 1951, the year I became a producer and was deep into my monastic life, I began to seriously keep what I call my spiritual diaries. I wouldn't put anything in them that wasn't a "click," wasn't something I felt deeply within. Mostly, I would keep my entries short and cryptic without rambling on. Often it would be weeks and sometimes months before I would make an entry. At other times when I was feeling spiritually fertile I would make entries every day for a week or two.

    In reviewing my diaries in preparation for writing this book, I was surprised to see that I was contemplating many of the same things then that I do today. Perhaps it has taken this long for thought to shift into conscious awareness at ever deepening levels. It isn't just repetitively going around in a circle over and over, but rather it is a kind of spiral that in returning expands higher and higher or deeper and deeper. Here are examples of a few of my entries:

> *When a soul is placed on the throne by God — God lives its life and one has no personal right to break the spiritual laws of love. One has no right to see anyone other than spiritually or one is violating the principle and not living up to faith or kingship.*

> *When doubts and misgivings precede an action, listen. It may be inner guidance. When doubts and misgivings follow an action, it is ego claiming the action was apart from God and is trying to sow to insecurity and duality.*

> *Faith is not just believing despite appearances. Faith is proceeding regardless of consequences.*

*Whenever Grace is withdrawn, it is pride which has cased its withdrawal—pride that would be if the feeling of Grace were not withdrawn.*

*Do not be concerned about how you relate to others. Maintain a conscious relationship with God and everything else will take care of itself.*

# The Hawaiian Years

In the late forties Joel went to Hawaii, initially because a Unity minister in Honolulu asked him to take over her pulpit for a month while she was in Europe. Joel moved into the Halekalani Hotel on Waikiki Beach in Honolulu, Hawaii, where he had a unique little room that stuck right out onto the beach. Though his official residence was still in Hollywood, he began to spend most of his time in Hawaii.

Joel seemed to blossom there. He came to feel that Hawaii was his spiritual home and he certainly appeared to be less driven and more relaxed there than on the mainland. His plaid coats and string ties gave way to flowered aloha shirts and sandals. He swam every day in front of the hotel and took to the aloha spirit with enthusiasm, even ending his letters from then on with "Aloha, Joel." Joel soon became friends with some of the traditional, native Hawaiian spiritual leaders, the Kahunas, and felt they had deep spiritual roots. In a way, Hawaii was an escape from the intense life in the states. Except to lecture, he knew he didn't want to return to the states and the consciousness he felt surrounded by there.

Nevertheless, during Joel's first year in the Islands, there were times when a wave of despair washed over him and he felt lost. Despite the good he had obviously done for so many and how his work had grown, part of him that he would never admit to felt that he was to some degree faking it. One night in his room on the beach he began to cry. With tears running down his face he called out to God saying that he was a failure. Then from within he heard, "Yes, Joel, you have failed, but I haven't! I will perform the work I will give you to do." After that he let go and knew he was where he should be.

When the Unity minister for whom he had substituted, returned, Joel did something that some would consider unethical. He hired a room nearby and started lecturing on his own. After having heard his sermons for a number of weeks, many of the Unity congregation began to attend and his following grew. The Unity minister so believed in Joel's message that she lovingly encouraged her people to go to his lectures, which were held at a different time than the Unity services.

Joel's lectures in Hawaii were recorded on an old reel-to-reel tape recorder. At an early meeting he asked for someone to run the recorder and to make copies of the tapes for people when they wanted them. Emma, an attractive and gracious lady in her forties who worked as a secretary in a beauty parlor, volunteered to run the machine. She had no way of knowing that within a year, producing tapes would become her full-time job, that when Joel moved to the other side of the island she would set up a studio in a home near his, and that eventually she would become Joel's fourth wife. Emma had come to Joel's lectures seeking a spiritual healing for her spastic son, Sammy, whose condition the doctors said was incurable. The boy was about 7 years old at that time.

I remember the first time I saw and met Emma and Sammy. Joel and I were sitting on the lawn behind the hotel at the water's edge around sunset one evening when we looked up and saw Emma and her son walking across the narrow sea wall that separated the Halekalani Hotel from the rest of Waikiki Beach and the Royal Hawaiian Hotel, with the waves crashing on one side and a ten-foot deep ditch on the other. I was alarmed because behind her was her spastic son, staggering down the wall, arms and legs flying in all directions, about to jerk himself off the wall onto the rocks below.

Though at that time the doctors said his condition was incurable, it took some years of working with Joel for Sammy's healing to fully take place. By the time he was in his teens there was no longer any sign of physical incapacity except for a very slight speech impediment, and he eventually became an airplane pilot.

When Joel was still living at the Halekalani, on some evenings five or six of us sat in wicker chairs on a grassy plot by the walk at the water's edge talking with him. At times the conversation would die down and we would lapse into a meditation. Meditation was not a popular custom in those days; so sometimes people would walk by, see us sitting there in stone silence with our eyes closed, and gawk at us as though we were freaks.

At least once a year I would return to Hawaii, sometimes accompanied by van Druten, and I would visit Joel. I ate, drank, and breathed his message. I was in awe of the power and energy I felt come through him. One day I was reading an article asking whether we would recognize Jesus if he were on Earth today, and as Joel taught that there is no unformed consciousness, I began to wonder if perhaps Joel was today's Jesus. When I was alone with him I sheepishly told him about my surmise, and although he must have heard me, he made no reply and abruptly changed the conversation.

Later, I realized that a physical presence wasn't what was significant to Joel, but rather the consciousness appearances represented. Whenever and wherever we recognize the Christ of another person, the Christ consciousness is present.

From my first meeting with Joel, through the Hawaiian days and during our times in New York and London, whenever I was present he automatically included me in every meeting, every meal, and every invitation he received. In Hawaii some of the most prominent people invited Joel to dinners and inevitably there would be a time when small talk would cease and Joel would hold us spellbound with his spiritual message.

Often in Joel's classes I was the youngest person present. One time I asked myself why that was so and my inner voice said, "You have to have this personal experience with Joel at your present age because of what you will be doing many years from now."

When Joel realized that he wanted to live in Hawaii permanently he rented a small apartment in a two-story wood duplex at the backside of Waikiki Beach looking out across a body of water called the Ala Wai. He turned one of the bedrooms into an office where he would spend time answering several dozen or more letters a day from people wanting healing and spiritual instruction. He would respond to every letter. As his work grew and the mail tripled, those around Joel became familiar with his constantly remarking, "I have to do the mail."

Joel would pick up a letter, read it, close his eyes for

a moment, turn to his Dictaphone and give a short answer, then he would pick up the next one. I would sit on the floor in the sparsely furnished office he had made out of his spare bedroom and listen to him dictate one after response the other. As he opened the letters money would rain out onto his desk in gratitude for his work and healings.

Although Joel did not charge for his healing work, he would meticulously note the five-and ten-dollar donations he received and declare them on his income tax, because that is what practitioners charged in those days. But anything over twenty-five dollars he considered to be a love gift and he didn't declare that. He did stretch the law a bit.

At the end of each of his replies to the letters, Joel would say, "I will be with you consciously every day." Hearing him repeat this over and over I thought, "What's he up to? How can he consciously be with hundreds of people every day?" So I asked him, "Joel, I have heard you say that same thing every day to countless people. Do you have a check-off list? How can you have that many people in your consciousness every day?" He answered, "I am with them every day because their true being is the Christ, and I am consciously with the Christ every day."

One time when I was in Hawaii we were invited to have lunch at a house of one of his followers in a residential area of fine old homes that looked down on Honolulu from the slopes of the old volcano behind the city. When we got out of the automobile in the driveway, close by was a little dog. I reached out to pet the dog, but he ran off as though threatened. Our host said they had taken the dog to the veterinarian, and after his stay there no one could get near him, not even his owners.

We went up onto the porch and sat down in comfortable white wicker porch chairs, waiting to be called in to lunch. After talking for a while, we decided to have a meditation. We all closed our eyes, and when I opened mine Joel's were still closed, but that dog had come up onto the porch and was sitting on his feet. The dog must have sensed Joel's healing power.

On that same trip I had a painful dog experience that was the opposite of the one I had witnessed with Joel. One day Joel told me that he was going to instruct me in the way spiritual power could be used or misused. He said that he would only teach this technique to students who were going to be teachers and involved in spiritual healing work. He cautioned against using it as witch doctors did to perpetuate their influence over people. It had to do with contacting the soul center of those who came for help. Joel said that I should never, never employ the technique unless absolutely necessary.

The next day I was sitting on the private beach that ran by the house I had rented out on Diamond Head when the neighborhood dog came on to the beach. I mistakenly thought that as the dog was not a human being it would be all right for me to see if the technique worked. The results not only turned out to be the opposite of my expectations, but it was a painful lesson for me.

Once I went into meditation with this intention in mind, the dog raced toward me, stopped ten feet away from me, and began to bark and bark as though he were warning everyone of something evil. I tried to calm him down but to no effect and he kept barking and barking, attempting to keep people away from me. Even with others trying to get him to stop, he wouldn't. Shaken, I went indoors to get away. After that, every time I came out on to the beach, if the dog was around, he would again rush over, circle about six feet from me, and begin to bark at me ferociously.

Finally, one day I was on the beach when the dog entered at the other end of the beach. Seeing me he started to race toward me. I closed my eyes, went into meditation, and swore that I would never again misuse what Joel had taught me. When I opened my eyes the dog was no longer running toward me. Instead he walked right by me as though I had ceased to exist and for the rest of my stay he continued to walk by me as though I were invisible.

Shortly after my dog experience I went back to New York. Though I continued to find work as an actor, it was becoming more difficult; my interest was more and more in the wider scope and intricacies of producing plays than acting in them. Besides that, I was becoming happier with who I was as a person, and I had less and less desire to take on the identity of, or put myself into the consciousness of, the characters I had to play as an actor. By this time I was further into my monastic period. My work with Joel had affected many changes in my consciousness, and I began to record them in my own words:

> *You have no love for your fellow man when you see him only as human.*

> *Every experience offers a chance for a constructive reaction.*

> *Heaven is a state of consciousness.*

> *Think not "I will be supplied"; I AM the supply.*

> *Your demonstration is your authority.*

*The secret is the impersonalization of good and evil.*

*It isn't that God is the only cause and by realizing that, things magically seem different; rather realizing oneness with cause makes cause operate as you.*

And it certainly did because things began to happen in my life that were unexpected blessings, and that changed the course of my life.

CHAPTER FIVE

# Producer Days

One night in New York van Druten called me from his ranch in California. He told me to go to the library and get a copy of Christopher Isherwood's *The Berlin Stories* and read the story called "Sally Bowles." He thought he might want to make a play out of it and wanted to know what I thought about it. After reading it I called John the next day and told him that I felt it was very risky, and perhaps way ahead of the times. The story was written in the first person and included a hint of homosexuality, Sally's abortion, and was set against the background of Hitler's Germany. None of these things were the subjects of plays in 1950. However, I added that it would be the kind of plotless character-driven play that I personally liked.

When I encouraged John to go ahead with the project, he invited me to come to his ranch to work on it with him and help him expand the short story into a full play. I told him that I had to meditate on it and would call him the next day with my answer.

That night I meditated long and hard. After a while, my inner voice said, "What do you want to do?" I answered, "I want to go out and work on the play." It responded, "Why don't you?" I answered, "Because my security is here in New York." It said, "That's the wrong reason."

In the late 1940s the television industry made a transition. Before that time the networks did all the casting of the TV plays, but then individual advertising agencies began to handle the casting and details of the shows their clients sponsored. Instead of an actor only having to stay in contact with the few network offices, he or she now had to visit many different agencies in order to become a familiar face and be ready to be called on a moment's notice.

I knew that if I dropped everything and went away for a length of time, I would lose ground and have to get everything going again on my return. When I told myself that I couldn't go to the ranch because my security lay in New York, my inner voice added, "Your security is within yourself." That settled it.

I made an appointment with Alfred Deliagra, Jr. who had produced John's highly successful *The Voice of the Turtle* and was going to produce his next play. I went to Deli's office the following day and asked him if I could be his assistant producer when John's next play was in production, which is a low-paying "gofer" job, but a way to learn the ins and outs of producing. Deli questioned, "Why do you want to do this? You are one of the few young actors on Broadway making top salary"—four times what I would get as an assistant producer. I answered that I didn't care because I wanted to learn the business. He said if that was my decision I could have the job; so I packed up and went to the ranch to work on the play with John.

Writing plays is not as time consuming as writing novels since a play consists of a couple of hours of dialogue at most. The technological aspects of a production were not John's areas of expertise; so one of my jobs was to design a floor plan and furniture placement that would help him, as the director, to block out the actors' movements around the set. Apart from that, I would help John with the script when he asked for my advice. We finished the play in several weeks, and sent it off to Deli in New York. I stayed on at the ranch to help with any changes and suggestions the producer might ask for.

A week later John, his business manager, Carter Lodge, and I were having lunch when the butler informed John that he had a telephone call, and he left the table to answer it. On his return a few minutes later, he told us that Deli and his wife hated the play. He said they thought it was the worst thing he had ever written, and said they had no doubt if produced it would ruin his reputation. John told them that he believed in the play and wanted to do it. Deli said that he was very sorry but he would not produce it.

Covering his disappointment with a stoic façade, John said, "What will I do now? I don't want to go back to Irene Selznick, and there isn't any producer I know that I like." Unexpectedly, Carter said, "Why not have Starcke produce it?" Without hesitation, John broke into a smile and exclaimed, "Yes! You do it." Needless to say, I was astonished and taken aback. My head was spinning as I said, "John, I can't jump from being a 30-year-old actor to producing a play for the top playwright on Broadway without more production experience." He rebutted, saying that I had proven myself on his other plays and my comments on the productions I had seen. After a few minutes excitedly contemplating all the ramifications, I arrived at a hopeful possibility. I said, "All right, if Gertrude Macy will co-produce it with me I will." Gert had given me my first job in the theater right after I got out of the Navy, and having produced a number of plays for the great actress, Katherine Cornell, could handle the details that were unfamiliar ground for me.

Of course, Gert jumped at the opportunity to produce a van Druten play, as almost any producer in New York would have. Before making it definite, because partnerships are tricky involvements, I went to New York to settle the contract and see how we could share authority. I meditated long and hard for answers and was rewarded with a concept that worked out beautifully. We decided that anything the audience could see was my territory—the set design and costumes, the actors, the publicity, and the play itself.

Gert was to be in charge of anything that took place behind the stage—hiring the company manager, negotiations with the theater owners, the actors' contracts, the unions, and raising the money. We would discuss all the details with each other, but if it came to a decision, the final say was up to the one whose area it fell into. John's play, set in pre-World War II Berlin, was *I Am a Camera*, which brought stardom to Julie Harris and won the New York Drama Critic's Circle Best Play Award for that year. Julie won the Tony for best Actress and Marion Winters for best supporting actress.

On opening night of *I Am a Camera* in 1951, Deliagra came to the play and after the curtain came down he went backstage and said, "What on Earth was I thinking? The play is an utter delight." I personally believe that God temporarily blinded Deli from seeing what the play could be because it was in the divine plan for me to produce it.

A few years after the Broadway run of *I Am a Camera*, the producer Hal Prince purchased the rights to make the play into a musical. The play, its plot and characters, became the basis for the smash hit musical and motion picture, *Cabaret*.

In those days, when people congratulated me for my successes, I smiled and thanked them, but inside I knew that I wasn't responsible. I listened to and followed my God-given intuition, and it showed me what to do. When I had these early successes it wasn't because I egotistically thought I could do it. It was because I didn't see any reason I couldn't.

After *I Am a Camera* opened, the novelist Adela Rogers St. Johns, who attended Joel's lectures and had a Christian Science background, went to see the play knowing that Joel had been giving us spiritual support during the production. Alarmed by what she thought was its immoral content, she wrote Joel a scathing letter about the play.

In the 1920s, William Randolph Hearst had built up Adela as the first powerful woman reporter in the country. She had single-handedly whipped up the American public against the Lindbergh kidnapping suspects, and, whether they were innocent or not, caused such a public uproar that they were convicted and executed. At one point she was Clark Gable's girlfriend, and when in Washington D.C. she was Huey P. Long's paramour. That is why I was surprised at the letter she wrote Joel telling him to stop praying for the play because it was vulgar and unworthy. In his typical sarcastic way, Joel wrote her back a tough letter telling her that if she thought his prayers to God could make something immoral successful, she didn't know anything about prayer.

As for moral codes, Joel was a perplexing person. He had his own invisible rules that had no humanly understandable standard. He would say one thing to one person and then the opposite to another. He could be completely non-judgmental towards someone's obviously shady morals or indulgences at one moment, and at another time he would frown, put on a stern face, and reprimand someone else for using an even slightly smutty word, particularly if that person was an Infinite Way student. He didn't emphasize morals in his public work, but with Victorian innuendo he would say that once you had a touch of spirit you would no longer be interested in gambling, playing cards, drinking, or promiscuity.

# Haleakala

$\mathcal{F}$resh from my success with *I Am a Camera,* in the summer of 1952 I went to visit Joel in Hawaii. Joel was giving his first week-long seminar in a hotel in downtown Honolulu and I came a week early to help him with the preparations.

The day after my arrival Joel took me over to the island of Maui, where he was to give a lecture and have private appointments with students. Some members of the all-important Baldwin family, descendents of the missionaries who ended up owning much of the island, were students of Joel's, and he had a number of devoted Hawaiian Japanese-American followers there as well.

We stayed in a two-storied old-fashioned Hawaiian-styled Japanese Hotel located near the port on the industrial side of the island. It had a tin roof, wide porches around each floor, and was painted dark green. While Joel was having private appointments on the first morning, I borrowed a car and drove up to see the giant Silver Sword flowers that bloom only in the crater atop Haleakala, the world's largest extinct volcanic crater.

The Hawaiians consider Haleakala the spiritual soul of the Islands; they say that the sun was born in the crater. As you climb toward the rim you start with tropical palm trees and flowering bushes and pass through just about every kind of climate and vegetation you can imagine until you rise above the clouds onto the barren walls of the crater.

No one told me that at the rim of the crater, ten-thousand-eight-hundred feet above the ocean, short pants and a tee shirt wouldn't do. I was freezing.

Hoping to get out of the cold wind I ignored the sign that said to stay on the path and climbed over the fence. In the rim of the crater I found a small body-size indention or cave-like space that would shelter me from the cold. The floor of the crater was blanketed in mist, so it was impossible to see the Silver Sword blossoms that grew there and nowhere else on earth. As I sat waiting for the mist to lift in this mysterious otherworldly place, I began to meditate and had the single most significant, life changing, and intense spiritual experience of my life.

It seemed as though I was hearing something like a tape recorded message playing in my head. The dialogue was on the subject of love. As all the different concepts of love flashed through my thoughts, I began to wonder, "We say we would love an ice cream cone; we love a sunset; we love our mothers; we love God. Are there different kinds of love? What really is love and what does it mean?" When I asked the question, images of Joel and Swami Prabhavananda, the two main teachers I was studying with, flashed through my mind.

Swami was the embodiment of everything I personally and esthetically appreciated. He had a gentle handsome face with eyes that showered everyone he looked upon with love. He dressed in elegant cashmere sweaters and fine linen slacks or he draped his chestnut gold body in a rich ocher robe. The décor, furnishings, and art work the Vedantists surrounded themselves with were the epitome of good taste. The lilting sound of the twelve-note Hindu music could be heard in the background, and brimming bowls of shiny fruit and nuts were always nearby.

The important thing about Swami is that he, similar to his surroundings, was extremely personal and he made each person feel special. When I came into his presence tears of joy at seeing me would well up into his eyes, and he made me feel not only loved but worthy of being loved. If I told Swami of my problems he would listen, understand, and be so personally concerned that my problems dwindled in importance. On the other hand, if I were to tell Swami that I had a physical problem such as a stomachache, he would care so much about my stomachache that I didn't mind having it any more—but when I left I most likely still had it.

Joel was another matter; he was almost totally impersonal. He was as happy to see you go as he was to see you come! He might let you tell him of your personal problem once so that you would get it off your chest but no more, and he most likely brushed the particulars aside as though they had no importance. However, if you rolled on the floor in pain the twinkle would leave his eyes, he would most likely grimace, and with a rather annoyed tone of voice say, "Get up, get up." The chances were that you would get up healed!

As I sat there in my cave waiting for the mists in the crater to clear and listening to my internal dialogue, I asked myself, "If the love I receive from Swami makes me feel good about myself and the love I get from Joel frees me from personal limitations and makes me feel I am more than human, which one of these do I want?" In a flash, I knew. "I want them both! I am a man of Earth who needs to be touched, loved, and appreciated, and I am also a man of God on his way to spiritual fulfillment who needs to be seen in his spiritual glamour, without limits, infinite, free to be anything he can imagine. I want love expressed both ways."

At that point a miracle happened. I became consciously aware of what is now, and actually always has been, the central theme of my life, what I now refer to as "The Double Thread." Everything I have written and tried to personally live ever since has followed from what I experienced on Haleakala. That spiritual breakthrough also tied my past religious conditioning to the present.

As with most church-going families at the time I was growing up, the Bible was a daily part of life; however, it had remained a closed book for me up until that epiphany. In the past I couldn't read the scriptures, but while sitting there contemplating the meaning of love, I saw or "heard" what I consider to be the secret of the New Testament. After that the Christian message was no longer a superstitious mystery. From then on its inherent wisdom opened like a flower, offering a practical philosophy of life that follows a definite pattern. At least it does if read without an overlay of man-distorted theological implications.

When I was contemplating the meaning of love that day I saw that, in instructing us about love, Jesus didn't give us just one commandment. He gave us two. He offered us an apparent duality, that when reconciled becomes One, or two commandments that when understood are "like unto each other." He said that if we added another commandment to the first one of the Old Testament we didn't need anything else, so for all practical purposes we can dispense with the other nine commandments of the Old Testament, the paranoid "thou shall nots." To the love of God, the first commandment, we should add the love of our neighbors as ourselves. Jesus concluded that in fulfilling those two commandments, all the laws or aims of the Old Testament would be fulfilled.

Sitting there in my cave I saw that the significance of these two commandments goes far beyond loving what one conceives God to be or what it means to love another human being. I saw that for all practical purposes the first commandment to love God really means that we should love "cause," the invisible source of life, and also that the second means we should love "effect," the visible or personal side of life. He added that if we love both cause and effect perfectly we will find that they are not only like each other but are also the same. I saw that the two commandments simply meant that at this human level nothing is either-or. I am not a man of Earth or a man of God. I am both, and, as a human being, my purpose in life is to make those two selves communicate with each other, two aspects of one being.

Before I left my cave that fateful day, I asked myself what Joel's healing secret was, and I was told that it was tantamount to the love of neighbor commandment, "Know ye no man after the flesh." I saw that Joel's capacity to see through material appearances and experience the impersonal spiritual truth of a person's being was how he healed people.

At the end of this profound experience atop Haleakala I drove down from the crater in time for lunch with Joel and some of his students. I didn't want to tell Joel of my experience until we were alone but did say that something important had happened. After lunch Joel continued to have appointments, and I took his suggestion that I drive up the nearby Iao Canyon to see the Needle.

The Needle is a towering monolith of volcanic rock standing free in the middle of a small canyon, isolated from the busy world just around the corner. Today there are parking places, paved walks, special observation spots, and hundreds of tourists, but at that time I was the only one there. I parked at the end of the road and walked up a narrow muddy path surrounded by dripping ferns and tropical plants until I found a rock where I could sit and meditate on the mysterious, more than human feelings that were overtaking me.

Sitting there in the cloud covered gloom, feeling chilled by the dampness, I suddenly thought how strange the situation was. Here there was misty oppressiveness and no evidence of an existing sun, while right around the corner it was blazing away in all its glory. I felt cut off from the world, alone, and out of touch with God. Then I heard, "You may not see it at this moment, but the sun is always shining. Not only that, but it has caused the clouds and produced the rain so that the beautiful flowers and lush growth can blossom in the canyon." Then I experienced the same life-changing tingle that I had felt earlier at the crater. I realized that whereas up at the crater I had discovered the meaning of the second commandment—how to love the material world of effect—here I was discovering how to love God. We love God when we know that, despite appearances, God, like the Sun, is always shining, is the only power, and the only cause.

My experience that day gave me the two tools that I was to spend the rest of my life learning how to use. I realized that the man of God and the man of Earth are simply two different dimensions of the one being that I am.

When my first book titled *The Double Thread* came out, some of Joel's students claimed that it was dualism, two threads. What they did not realize is that in reality it is one thread made up of two strands, the human and the divine, and that two strands woven together are much stronger than the sum of two individual strands standing alone.

After my fantastic day, I couldn't wait to get back with Joel to tell him what I had experienced. That night after his talk, Joel and I returned to the hotel. He had been given a big bowl of tropical fruit by one of his students, and after a discussion of the day's happenings he suggested that I take some of it with me to my room. I chose a nice plump mango. Back in my room I didn't have anything with which to peel it; so I bit into its thick skin, peeled it back, and ate the delicious fruit. No one had told me to watch out, because Mango skins have the same chemical composition as poison ivy.

I woke up the next morning with my eyes swollen almost shut and my lips blown up like balloons. I was supposed to join Joel for breakfast. When I arrived, with a child-like pathetic voice, I pleaded, "Why did this happen to me? I just had the most important spiritual experience of my life." Joel paused and then replied, "You can't eat two big meals one on top of the other," meaning that I had just had a spiritual banquet and was about to have another at the class in a few days. "This will purge you and get you ready," he added. When we returned to Oahu there was excitement in the air. A meeting room was reserved at the Roosevelt Hotel in downtown Honolulu, preparations were being made for the seminar, and people from all over the world were arriving.

The day I returned to Honolulu I received a call from my mother telling me that she wanted to attend the seminar. I was disturbed about it and said I would call her back. Though I felt very close to my mother, after my father died when I was nine she centered too much attention on her only son. I did all that I could to escape the emotional attachment. After the war I would visit her for a week or two a year but always had my return ticket so that I could escape if necessary. When I told Joel about mother's call, that she really didn't know what was in his teaching, and that I thought she was coming just to get involved in my life, he said, "That's not for you to decide. If she isn't supposed to get here she won't." Well, she got there!

I had once more rented the little cottage out on Diamond Head where I had previously had the dog experience, and mother came to stay with me. I invited Joel and a dozen or so of the inner circle from the mainland to come for a fruit juice cocktail party on the afternoon of the first talk. This group, almost all women, was composed of charming but very impersonal and reserved long-time metaphysicians. They weren't physically demonstrative and, in fact, hardly even shook hands. I was embarrassed, because mother took it on herself to be a typical southern hostess, full of small talk and studied charm. I was relieved when the party was over and I could concentrate on preparing for that evening.

Joel had asked me to lead the meditations on the opening night. As he had said that meditations should be spontaneous and unrehearsed spiritual messages, after the party I spent the afternoon on the private beach meditating to get myself out of the way. Getting on top of my ego wasn't easy because there were a number of people from several countries there, all older than I, and I considered it not only an honor but a responsibility to fulfill Joel's trust. When the time came that night I mumbled something about the Scripture telling us to eat of Jesus' consciousness and drink of his spirit. However, I didn't feel I was very inspired or even coherent, but Joel seemed satisfied, and by the time his exhilarating talk was over I was walking on air.

On the way home in my rented auto, mother was very quiet. Then she suddenly blurted out, "What's this going to do with my past beliefs?" I told her that that was precisely the point; this was a new way of looking at life and she had to choose whether to live by the laws the church set down or by her own inner guidance. She then asked me something about the need to forgive. I told her the impersonal principle, and what it does to one's self if one does not forgive, but she personalized it and took it as though I was judging her for not forgiving, applied it to herself, and said, "Now listen here young man don't you tell me … etc." When she did that it brought me down from my spiritual high with a bang. It was like puncturing a hole in a balloon. She was doing just exactly what I had feared she would do, and I was furious. I don't recall my ever having talked to my mother in anger before, but this time I shouted, "Shut up! You don't know what you are talking about; so just shut up." We drove the rest of the way home in fuming silence, and when we got to my cottage mother went off to her room in a huff. I put on my pajamas and went out onto the terrace to meditate and clear my feelings.

In a few minutes I heard from within, "The greatest act of love that we can do for another person is to help them find God. Everything a psychiatrist might say that your mother should not have done has driven you to become who you are today. After the war it drove you to go to New York rather than back to Texas, drove you to find answers, and ultimately drove you to find God; so everything she has ever done has been an act of love."

At that exact moment my mother came to the door, stood there for a moment, and said, "I see." I replied, "See what?" In a soft and awestruck voice she answered, "I have always thought that you are my son. You are not! You are a child of God like we all are. What's more, I think you are my teacher."

From that moment on, for the remaining seventeen years of my mother's life, we had a most wonderful relationship. I would visit her for a month or more at a time without the everlasting arms trying to pull me back again. After her Hawaiian visit she attended a number of Joel's classes, was included in the first meeting of the special Group of 25 that Joel addressed at a New York class, and she got a group together in San Antonio to hear Joel when he visited us there.

Mother stayed active and busy right up until she passed on at 87 after only a couple of days in the hospital. On my last visit with her I took away with me a card I found on her desk written in her handwriting and read it to her. On one side it said:

> *Fill me today with all thou art. Fill me with thy soul, with Thy spirit, with Thy grace that my presence on earth may show forth Thy glory, which I had with thee before the world was' the original glory of divine Sonship.*

*John 17:5*

On the other side:

> *Thou art my day. Thou art my night. Thou art the wisdom that guides and governs me. Thou art the soul that purifies my every thought and deed. Thou art the spirit that purifies every motive and makes of me givingness.*

These were the last words I spoke to my mother. Today I carry that card with me in my Bible along with a picture of Joel.

As a direct result of my mother's visit to Hawaii, a visit I had initially dreaded, I learned that as human beings we cannot know the why or wherefore of our experiences. But if we truly turn ourselves over to the Spirit and practice the principles that we honor, whatever is needed in the process of our spiritual evolution will take place.

My determination to live what I had learned at Joel's side and my continuing absolutism is reflected in some of my diary entries I made at that time.

*Nothing in the dream matters. To take thought for the future is to anticipate the dream.*

*Life is a dream. I do not exist, Joel does not exist, Jesus does not exist. Only God, I, am. I am always returning unto myself. Individual will is only in the less-than-absolute—in the dream. God is not in the dream and does not change the dream.*

*"I" means God.*

*St. Theresa: "If I am to love you as you love me, I must borrow your love; I can find no other love any other way." Any love—spiritual seeing—in me is proof of Oneness for I am love.*

*Perhaps my desires are only a dream and nothing but folly. If so, I beg you make it clear to me, because you know I seek the truth. If my desires are over bold, then take them away, because they are my greatest martyrdom.*

*Not "he is God," rather, "God is his being." God is as me—as I am. Heaven and earth are the same place. Thank you father.*

*For God so loved me that he gave me Joel so that I might be saved, but he gave me Joel, not to condemn me, but to save me.*

*You will never see man perfectly or spiritually. You may only be aware of man spiritually. Walter Starcke will never be flawless—I already am. The disciples saw Jesus as perfect, others did not. To them he ascended, but not to human sense. It is impossible to see anyone lacking duality unless you see them as Christ. This you cannot try to do. Don't try to see man as Christ, it is impossible. The soul of every man is spiritual, and every soul will ascend.*

# The Vedanta Turning Point

A few days after the class in Hawaii, mother returned to Texas and I prepared to leave for California to be present at the Vedanta monastery on the Fourth of July for Vivekananda's death-day celebration. Often in India they celebrate death days instead of birthdays. Because they don't believe that life ends with death, they celebrate the incarnation one has just lived. Vivekananda's death day is the one day of the year that women are allowed to visit the monastery.

The morning I left Hawaii, Joel and several of his students took me to the airport to send me off. He put a powerfully-perfumed pekaki lei around my neck and surprised me with an affectionate Hawaiian embrace. I could hardly see out from under the blanket of flower leis he and his students had piled upon me to wish me aloha. On the plane the stewardess passed out plastic bags for the passengers to put their leis in so that they would stay fresh during the long propeller plane flights of that time.

When I arrived in Los Angeles, van Druten was at the airport to meet me and drive me down to the monastery for the celebration. I arrived laden down with nine bags of leis! Swami was overjoyed because in India copious flower garlands adorn the statues and the gurus during such celebrations. He believed that I had been thoughtful enough to buy the leis for the occasion; it surely was an example of Divine synchronicity.

After the celebration, John left and I stayed on at the monastery for a few days. On the third morning I had a particularly deep meditation that lasted for over an hour. Swami was the only person left in the sanctuary when I finished and went to the little room at the entrance where you leave your shoes. I was putting mine on when Swami came in. During the meditation I had felt a strong desire to find out what the mantra would be for "I am that I am," or, in substance, "I am God." There alone with Swami in the shoe room I asked him what the Sanskrit for such a mantra would be. He got tears in his eyes and said, "I've lost you." He then told me it was "Aham Brahmasmi," the mantra given when a monk is initiated as a swami after a minimum of eight years of study.

Swami had always felt that perhaps I would be among the first Americans to become a swami in his order. I think he said he had "lost me" because he realized that I had arrived at the realization that my true being is the presence of God in another way. Actually, I believe that my work with Joel and the experience I had on Haleakala had taken me there.

After Swami told me the mantra, I asked him to spell it for me, but I had nothing to write it on. I looked through my wallet and the only thing I could find was a passport photo of Joel that he had given me; so, ironically, I wrote it on the back of Joel's picture.

Though I saw Swami a few times after that visit, our relationship was never quite the same. After my experience on Haleakala I saw spiritual healing as an act of grace rather than a result of karmic law, the way much of Standard Hinduism does. Ramakrishna, the Vedanta saint, died in great pain and though they say he did not mind, I wasn't satisfied with their conclusion. Their explanation is that by healing others Ramakrishna had taken on their karmic pains. Each time I was with Swami Prabhavananda after that experience I would feel tremendous gratitude for the important, loving, and helpful wisdom he would offer so generously, but in the end the subject of spiritual healing seemed to stand like a wall between us. My visits became less frequent, and I was in Europe and unable to attend his services when he died a few years later.

Haleakala, The Creater

Swami Prabhavanada

The photo of Joel Walter carried in his wallet. Swami's mantra, "Aham Brahmasmi," is hand written on the back.

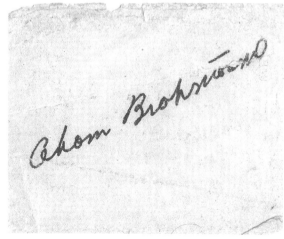

CHAPTER SIX

# The New York Years

*E*arly in 1953, I stayed a full two months in Hawaii with Joel and spent hours listening to him dictate his letters, attended his lectures, and dined with him almost every day. During this time I began to learn more about what went on beneath the surface of this complicated multi-dimensional man.

The few people with whom Joel would share his private world were those he felt would accept his personal self without losing sight of his spiritual being. Though he taught impersonalization, we also loved him because of his humanity. We loved Joel because we saw the intense difficulty he had in coping with the world of personal sense. That was the price he paid for offering us a way that could help us better cope with it ourselves. We loved him because despite his feeling that he was called to do this important work, there was a childlike innocence that at times showed itself, as it does in most great masters. And we loved him because at a critical moment his sly sense of humor would keep us from taking things too seriously.

Sometimes Joel's humor would carry a tinge of New York sarcasm beneath it. For instance, one time a group of people from California offered to put up an enormous amount of money to create, publicize, and promote an organization or foundation to support his Infinite Way teaching. Instead of politely refusing them, his sassy human side came out and he said, "Fine, go ahead, but I will be the only one who has a vote," and, of course, that was that. There was no way Joel would allow others to control or influence his message.

No matter how many of us went out for a snack with Joel after a talk or to dinner, he was always generous. When the check came, if you wanted it to be your treat you had to be quick on the draw, because he would insist on paying the bill.

In order to get a feel for the man, Joel, it is important to listen to some of his tape-recorded lectures, the tapes from which Lorraine Sinkler fashioned his books. His spirit, humanity, and humor would reach out from the tapes much more powerfully than the words did on paper. Unfortunately, Lorraine did not have a sense of humor, and in editing the tapes to turn them into books much of Joel's wit was left out. In person he always got a youthful twinkle in his eye when his cunning humor expressed itself. He often smiled and said that the reason he began his tape recordings by saying, "Good evening," was because he didn't want those hearing the tapes to think he was talking to himself.

In writing *The Spiritual Journey of Joel. S. Goldsmith*, following what she believed Joel wanted, Lorraine's intent was to keep her account as impersonal as possible. She felt that there was to be "a minimum of factual data because that was not the measure of the man: what counted was what he was and his work. Always, the work was the most important consideration to him. Joel knew that someday someone would write his life story and he hoped it would be written by a person who had been close enough to him to understand his work."

Just when you thought that Joel was beyond caring about what anyone thought, he would reveal a very human humility. Sometimes after his talks, when we were alone, in a plaintive voice he would ask me, "Was I all right tonight?" He would usually ask such questions on the very nights when he was at his very best and his message most profound. Perhaps he felt helpless on those nights because he was so taken over by the Spirit that he hadn't been personally in charge.

Joel wasn't so absolute that he didn't need approval from those he loved. When Joel bragged about how the Infinite Way and his writings were spreading and receiving recognition around the world, underneath his words was a grateful note of self-satisfaction for having personally fulfilled his mission on Earth. On the other hand, Joel once told me, "I have been a failure at everything in life except for one thing—staying on the path."

Joel didn't brag on himself nor was he falsely humble, yet one day he surprised me by acknowledging his unique calling and importance by saying that the people sitting next to him on an airplane trip had no idea who or what was sitting beside them.

In practice Joel was more human and less absolute than his teaching implied, or that his Christian Science background advocated. In several of his lectures he stated that there were times that he would not eat meat; however, I never saw him turn down a good steak. His favorite restaurants were not those that offered gourmet French cuisine but rather those where he could get a juicy thick sirloin.

Showing a clear break from Christian Science absolutism—Joel loved a cup or two of coffee throughout the day, and I got him to have a sherry or a glass or two of wine with dinner. Without attributing cause to effect, he swallowed the daily vitamins Emma gave him. Though I never felt he planned for or depended on them, Joel enjoyed the so-called better things in life.

In talking about the impersonal nature of life and relationships, Joel implied that we could rise above the ordinary need for personal contact with loved ones, yet when he was on the road alone before and after he married Emma, he would call her every night to make contact.

Joel handled big issues of life impeccably, but sometimes he would react humanly to small irritations. I was with him one day in Hawaii when an FTD bouquet of wilted flowers that were obviously being recycled arrived from the florist. Joel was so incensed by the flower shop's lack of integrity that he called up the Better Business Bureau and reported them.

Unfortunately I did not follow it, but when Sammy, Emma's son, was in his teens he gave me the most sage advice about how to deal with Joel, the man. I complained about having a minor misunderstanding with Joel, and Sammy said, "If you do something that annoys Joel don't try to appease him. Make him mad and he will turn it over to God." Joel handled everything he could metaphysically. He seldom gave direct orders, but instead he would announce a need and someone always volunteered to take care of it. In all my years with him he rarely outright required any thing or any action from me. Instead, I tried to anticipate areas where I could be of assistance and volunteered.

Joel's super-critical eye intimidated me and most of his other students, not because he did or said anything judgmental but because we wanted his approval so much that we feared not receiving it. Lorraine, in particular, seemed continuously anxious, if not cowed, in his presence, afraid that she might not live up to his expectations.

Joel is difficult to analyze in psychological terms. He danced to a different drummer. Despite the fact that he was very knowledgeable in many areas, he really didn't live by logic. He lived totally by instructions from his inner guidance, which turned out to be very logical when the results were in place, but not necessarily so at the time he initiated his actions. Because of his passion to transcend the level of personal sense, I believe that, like all of us, he wasn't always in touch with his own feelings.

You had to be pretty self-confident to disagree with Joel or to challenge him. On any subject, spiritual or not, Joel made his pronouncements with the same authority and conviction that he did when expounding on spiritual matters. When he was commenting on spiritual subjects he was pure truth, but his advice wasn't always valid when speaking on other subjects.

I remember watching television with him one night when a young Shirley Temple clone performed a song and dance number. Joel emphatically proclaimed, "Now there is a future star." Theater was my area of expertise, and I knew we would never hear from her again. Of course we didn't.

Apart from Joel's spiritual convictions, the other matter on which he left no space for any equivocation or disagreement was on the subject of politics. Over the years I learned to avoid the subject, because he would make his pronouncements with such Old Testament fervor that I felt disagreeing with him would mean, "Off goes your head."

President Franklin D. Roosevelt dominated all of my formative years and to me he was the great white father, but to Joel he was the devil's handyman. At that time I couldn't understand why Joel was so adamant in his disapproval of Roosevelt. Years later I realized that Roosevelt, the man, wasn't what disturbed Joel; rather it was the social security consciousness he exemplified. Joel felt that social security laid the groundwork for a big brother form of government and that once we started looking for the government to take care of us we would lose respect for ourselves and for our freedom. More importantly, we would stop turning within for our good.

Joel did not publicly talk about the full range of psychic phenomena that he had personally experienced, except to explain the principles to his closest students. He alerted them to the danger of practicing an approach which they might be caught between the material and spiritual levels of consciousness. He said that phenomena were just what the word said—phenomenal, not necessarily bad or destructive, but just not a mystical or spiritual activity. To whatever degree psychics were still affected by personal sense would color and influence their messages.

Joel's mystical approach was so absolute and pure that a number of psychics asked him to protect them from taking on some of the transferences that were the result of their more mental approach. Eileen Garrett, the most popular and well known psychic alive during the 1940s, came to Joel for counseling and healing because she believed he was a pure mystic and the only one she felt could help her keep from being caught in the astral plane—a place between the tangible world and the spiritual plane.

Joel did believe in reincarnation and he told me that perhaps he was a reincarnation of Paul. I can see how that would apply. In his teaching, like Paul's, Joel would spend the majority of his time addressing the shortcomings and foibles of our human nature, and then without explaining that he was now referring to our spiritual nature, he would tell us of our true existence from a purely mystical standpoint beyond the need for redemption.

Though Joel didn't include discussions about the possibility of having guides from what he called "the other side" in his meditations and lectures, he personally had several guides or states of consciousness that he felt came to him at times. Mary Baker Eddy was one and Jesus was another. There was also Paul and an oriental master. Those of us who attended many of his classes, and I went to 33, reached a point when we could sometimes recognize which consciousness he was tuned into. When he was absolute and in denial of the material world, it was Mrs. Eddy; when he approached spirituality from the limitations of our human side, it was Paul; and when he was making statements that were impersonal and subjective, his oriental consciousness took over. At the high point of his mystical meditations he felt that the pure Christ consciousness was speaking through him. Sometimes during a lecture I sensed a slight change in his manner and later asked him if at that exact time he had been experiencing one of his guides. I was usually right in suggesting which one. Sometimes I believed that I saw a shadowy presence standing behind him as he spoke.

As a human being, Joel lived with a kind of spiritual Muzak playing in the background of his awareness. Through meditation he would get the music tuned in and then go about his daily activities without consciously thinking about it; however, if the subconscious music stopped he would instantly become aware that it had, and he would drop everything to meditate once more and get the music playing again.

I remember one night in Hawaii when van Druten was there and several of us went to a Japanese restaurant for dinner. All of a sudden in the middle of dinner Joel got up, excused himself, said he would be back, and went out into the garden alone. After a while he returned and explained that someone who had urgently asked for a healing came into his consciousness; so he had to go and make his inner contact. His spiritual ministry was always at the forefront of his mind.

Joel's favorite time to meditate was around three o'clock in the morning at which time he felt the world consciousness around him was at its quietest. He would automatically wake up at that time and meditate. Though Joel did not want the intimacy of students living on his premises or a too-personal relationship, he wrote that he wished teachers in the West would do the same as Hindu swamis who had their students live with them so that if the Swami had a spiritual inspiration in the middle of the night he could send word for them to come right away and then go back to bed after he had talked to them.

All in all, Joel was a driven man. He was not a man with a message. He was a message with a man. He was pushed into sharing the message wherever there was anyone to listen, night or day. The size of the group made no difference. Protecting the integrity of his work was always uppermost in his mind. Joel made no secret of the fact that the people with whom he surrounded himself were without exception those who could and would do the most for his work.

It was obvious that Joel made an extra effort with celebrities and people who were in positions of prominence and wealth who could help support and foster his teaching. He paid special attention to Barbara Muhl, whose husband was the head of Universal Pictures for many years. He courted

Olney Flynn and his wife, who owned oil fields in Oklahoma. He had asked van Druten, a celebrity whom he had known for only a short time, to write the introduction to *The Infinite Way*. On the other hand, all of these students were also highly evolved and worthy of his attention. There, too, his impersonal nature showed itself because his interest was not in personality but in what those personalities represented and what they could do for his work.

Though Joel was generous with the time and effort he put into teaching me, there was an explanation that revealed the impersonal nature of our relationship. I once asked Joel why he gave me so much. He answered, "Because you ask for so much."

# The Divine Curse

*D*uring my two months in Hawaii, I felt I really came to know Joel at a more intimate level than just his public persona. I didn't hold back any of my thoughts or feelings and felt closer to him and more like family than ever before. On my return to New York I began to feel frustrated. John hadn't written a new play since *I Am a Camera* and I couldn't find any other plays that I wanted to produce. I had an option on the play *Anastasia*, which eventually became a Broadway hit and later a movie with Ingrid Bergman, but I let it go. Even though I knew it would be financially successful, I just wasn't interested in doing something just for money. With no new prospects on the horizon, I went with John to London to help with the final casting of the London production of *The King and I*, which he was to direct. On that trip something happened that set the course for the rest of my life.

After the casting was over, John and I had a couple of weeks to kill before rehearsals were to start; so we decided to visit the mainland and tour around. We rented a car in Paris, drove down to the Riviera, on to San Sebastian, Spain, and started up the west coast. A national strike broke out in France; so we dropped off the car and took a train straight through to Amsterdam where we had reservations at the Amstel Hotel.

Our mail had been forwarded to us at the hotel; so after we put our luggage in our rooms we went to the desk and inquired. I was handed a packet of letters and was pleased to see one from Joel on top. I sat down in the lobby, opened it, and began to read. Half way through I broke into tears. Alarmed at my reaction, John asked me what was wrong. Too full of emotion to speak I mumbled, "Nothing. I will be back in a minute," and went to my room to pull myself together and try to understand what had happened.

For some months I had been feeling that I wasn't making any spiritual progress. My meditations seemed forced; I felt completely empty as though I was just marking time. I seriously questioned whether I really had a calling for the spiritual life and felt that perhaps I had been kidding myself. Joel's letter changed that forever. The impact of his words left me no doubt as to my longing. When I read the letter I felt the equivalent of having come face to face with a long-lost love that I had been searching for all of my life. A door opened in my soul and the light flooded in, the light of love. It showed me where home was, and I knew that from then on the purpose of my life would be the journey homeward. I didn't know where the path would take me, but I knew my hunger to experience the presence of God was all that mattered from then on. I knew without a doubt that I had to totally immerse myself in the mystical approach to life. It was as though Joel had laid a kind of benevolent or divine curse on me that set the pattern for the rest of my life.

To this day I carry a copy of Joel's letter in my Bible. I would like to show the letter written by Joel's hand, but as that is not allowed I will translate it to the best of my ability. It was written on August 12, 1953 at 2:25 in the morning.

After the usual "Dear Walter" salutation he said "As you will sometimes learn, this is the holiest night of my life." He said that in the middle of this night of wonderful revelation, I had come to mind from something I had written to him in a recent letter, to the effect that I wanted something to do—some activity—some work—something to keep me occupied—and that this answer was given to him: "Walter, why don't you make me (God) your activity—your occupation—your way of filling the time? Why not let me (God) fill your days & nights—your mind, soul, and body?" He told me not to seek occupation or activity, that I was to seek God and that God would fulfill me. He said that God would fulfill me and be sufficient for me. And all the things will be added.

He said that the Spirit told him I was called to Mysticism—that my whole being must be filled with God.

Joel wrote that our work is so little understood because people look at him and think that the Infinite Way is just a job, a way of earning money. They do not see that his "consciousness" is filled with God around the clock, "that God is really my being, not merely a subject for classes."

Joel wrote that it is necessary that the outer life "be normal, natural, as far as people knew, but even tho it is not understood by material sense. our inner lives must be not mine but His—our being must be not I—but Him."

He ended the letter saying, "He is the air we breathe, the food we eat, the sleep we sleep, the love we love—the life we live," and he added that "it had not been told me to write this or tell this to any other student," but that I was free to share it with John whenever I felt the desire.

Today, 50-plus years later, though Joel's letter is long since committed to memory, whenever I feel inadequate or think that I should be doing something I am not presently doing, I pick up a copy and read it over again. It releases me from all personal concerns and Joel's presence becomes as real to me as it was the day I burst into tears in the lobby of the Amstel Hotel.

# The New York Classes

When I returned from London, Joel wrote me that he wanted to give a public lecture in New York followed by a class that fall. I reserved the ballroom in the Roosevelt Hotel for the lecture and a separate room for the class to follow. I am not sure how Joel had acquired his mailing list, but over two hundred people showed up for the lecture and thirty or forty attended the class. This was Joel's first New York appearance, so I was especially honored when he asked me to personally introduce him. By this time, in public Joel's plaid coats and aloha shirts had given way to dark gray suits with black string ties.

Years later in some of Joel's lectures he would mention this first class and the evening when there was a great racket caused by the emptying of some trash cans in the hall outside the classroom. I remember it well, because when that happened Joel turned directly to me, made a face that told me to see that it be stopped. I felt personally responsible for the ruckus as though it were entirely my fault.

In later years, Joel would share some of his personal feelings with a few of his inner circle, but on this first talk in New York, I was the only one around who had spent time with him in Hawaii and elsewhere; so when he had a couple of disturbing telephone calls from Nadea, his wife, before and during the class, he confided it to me at a more personal level than he ever had before. By discerning the spiritual reason for Joel's painful experience I learned a lesson that helped me years later when I began to lecture publicly.

Nadea's disturbing calls were the result of a conflict that had been building for some time. As Joel fell in love with Hawaii and began to spend more and more time there, Nadea began to pull away. She didn't want to give up her own practice in Hollywood or leave the Christian Science Journal. To join him in Hawaii she would have had to do so. These issues deepened, and Nadea and Joel's conversations became more caustic.

The crisis point was reached the night of the New York class when she called Joel and informed him that she had filed for divorce and stated her demands. Joel was angrier at her having called and disturbed him just before his talk than at her wiping him out financially. According to Joel, she wanted everything he had, and as he had sworn never to go to court again there was no alternative than to give in to her. When the divorce came through Joel was once more left with only a few thousand dollars in his bank account.

The lesson I learned from Joel's disturbing experience was that often preceding any of our most significant breakthroughs or important appearances, such as Joel's first New York talk, personal sense and our egos conjure up something that can potentially break our concentration and distract us from being at our best. If we understand that such situations are temptations, we can use them rather than being used by them. If, in having to cope with negative energy, we of necessity go deeper within ourselves, the experience might well result in our bringing forth an even more profound message. That was the price Joel paid for his stunning initial talk in New York.

As a result of Joel's first talk in New York, something else significant happened that eventually led to Harper & Row publishing Joel's books. Frances Steloff created and owned the famous Gotham Book Mart, then on 47th Street, a favorite meeting place of many of the greatest writers of the 20 Century. Frances was practically dragged to the lecture by a friend, but after hearing Joel's talk, she became one of his most ardent followers.

Frances, who lived to be a hundred years old, was a fascinating little Jewish woman with only a high school education, but she was responsible for helping many of our most important writers get their first works published, among them James Joyce, Ernest Hemmingway, and many others. Frances' self-cut gray hair was always in a state of disarray with strands escaping her cap-like headgear. She wore clunky, earthy, health shoes, undistinguished cotton blouses, faded flowered skirts, and was strictly vegetarian.

In the back of her store Frances had a little niche where she sat on a stool surrounded by Joel's books and his picture. Many times you would find famous writers standing there paying court. Frances provided room in the back of her store for me to conduct what soon became Joel's largest weekly tape recording group.

Our group met on Wednesday evenings. I would read two or three of Joel's "Wisdoms;" those that ended up being printed in the later copies of *The Infinite Way*. I would comment on them briefly to get everyone centered, and follow up with a meditation. Then we would listen to a tape of one of Joel's talks. At Joel's request, at the end of the tape there was no discussion; we would simply mumble our good-byes and leave.

On one of Joel's visits to New York, he met with the group in person and spoke for an hour on each of two consecutive evenings. Because most members of the group were new to the Infinite Way, Joel gave the most comprehensive, clear, and concise summation of his message and the subject of meditation that I have come across in any of his recordings. At the conclusion of the second hour, he gave me the tape and signed it as "A gift to Walter." After Joel's death, I gave the tape to Joel's tape department so the public could have access to it. He had titled it *The Gotham Tape*. There is no finer introduction to and brief discourse on *The Infinite Way*.

From 1953 until the early 1960s, Joel left all the details of his New York lectures and classes up to me. I organized the notices, negotiated for and acquired the meeting rooms, paid the bills, and collected the tuitions for his seminars. Joel didn't want to be bothered with any of the production side. He never questioned me, but always said, "Just give me what is left over." For five days of four-hour-a-day classes, he charged only $25, which was very little even then. His goal wasn't to make money from his lectures. He told me that unless those who attended didn't value what was taking place enough to pay something, they wouldn't complete the circle and receive anything.

Joel had absolute integrity when it came to his work. He honestly didn't care about numbers of people. He gave as much to a dozen as to a thousand. He felt that the masses were not ready for his message, and he didn't want to attract people by offering them the "land of milk and honey." He believed that without elaborate promotions or advertising the Spirit would lead those to him who were ready to hear what he had to say, and it did.

Joel would allow a small notice to be put in the paper saying that Joel Goldsmith would talk on *The Infinite Way,* but not that it was about healing, supply, or any of the catchwords that would bring people in for material reasons. In no way did he ask audiences for money, either for his healing work or to cover meeting expenses. At the public lectures a bowl would be placed at the door for those who wanted to put in a love offering, but no announcement would be made of that fact.

The classes ran from Monday through Friday nights with two-hour morning and evening sessions and the afternoon off. They were called closed classes, because no one was allowed to participate if they were not there from the beginning. Joel's aim was to build a consciousness and a sense of oneness within the group, and that cohesion would be interrupted if others were allowed to join after the first night.

At first, Joel would have an early morning meeting made up of a few practitioners and his more serious inner circle. He told us he had these special sessions in order to say things that the general public was not ready for; however, after a few years he changed his mind and said that he had come to realize "I can say whatever the Spirit tells me to say and those who are not ready to hear it will only hear what they are capable of hearing."

Joel did not speak from notes or written material. He meditated for hours before a lecture to find out what direction to take and let the consciousness of the group draw forth what they needed. He might take along an article he wanted to quote, but he depended completely on his inner voice to come forth with the message, and, as though it had been planned that way, the message would come out with a beginning, a middle, and an end. His lectures were recorded on hour-long tapes and would inevitably last exactly an hour before we would take a break.

One time in Chicago I had been meditating with Joel in his hotel suite before the talk. In the elevator on our way to the lecture hall he helplessly said, "I have nothing to say. I just have nothing to say. Nothing has come to me. I don't know what is going to happen." When he got on the platform he shut his eyes, meditated a bit, and began repeating a few of his standard statements. Then all of a sudden he stopped, opened his Bible, and said, "I will now read from the Sermon on the Mount." Joel had never used this particular Scripture before in his lectures, nor had he written about it, but that night he proceeded to give one of the most important messages of his career!

Those attending Joel's classes were asked to come half an hour early, to enter silently, and to meditate until he began. My job was to greet old friends at the door, help with those registering, and deal with last minute details. Near the end of the meditation, Joel would come in quietly, sit down behind a table in front, and glance at the questions that had been placed there. He then closed his eyes for just a minute, nodded at whoever was running the tape recorder, and without any fanfare begin to speak. He spoke softly, without any fireworks. He never shouted, raised his voice, or made dramatic gestures, and yet you could hear a pin drop as all of us were held spellbound. One had the feeling that Joel was simply the pipeline through which a higher source was speaking.

I always sat close to the entrance once the lecture started. Sometimes I had to wrap my feet around the legs of my chair, because Joel would say something that would cause me to experience a flash of truth that almost jolted me off the chair. After precisely one hour, Joel would have us take a ten minute break. Before he began the second hour he shuffled through the written questions that had been placed on his table during the break and then began again, usually by answering some or all of the questions.

Joel never explained why he wouldn't take questions directly from the floor. I concluded that it was for two reasons. First, he wanted to put aside any frivolous questions and sort the rest into some kind of order or sequence before addressing them. Second, he wanted to keep his work impersonal, without bringing attention to the personality of the one who had asked the question in person.

Some of my fondest memories are of the intimate times we had after Joel's talks. I always booked us into meeting rooms around the Carnegie Hall area. Every night after we finished, Joel, one or two of his inner circle, and I would go out for coffee and a blintz at the Russian Tea Room on 57th Street, a favorite spot of Joel's. He was usually in high spirits from the lecture and bubbled with talk. We would laugh a lot and share our appreciation of the evening. Joel was at his most personal and humorous at those times. When the coffee or food arrived he would always smile, raise his eyebrows, and say, "Happy days."

As time went on, I realized how important this inner circle was to Joel. It wasn't just the visible support and encouragement that we gave him: it was much more than that. We were all hooked up at some inner spiritual level, and somehow our energies enhanced Joel's. Where two or more are gathered together in the same consciousness, that consciousness is more evident. After the morning session I would return to my office, and about mid-afternoon before the evening lecture I would begin feeling a strong "pull" that compelled me to leave my office and go to my apartment to meditate. That evening, somewhere in the middle of the talk, I would feel a release as though I was now floating in a stream and my energy was no longer being called upon.

Joel was sometimes disappointed with an audience's reaction to what he had said. I remember one time in New York after the public lecture he said to me, "No one heard me. I just said something that cuts right across metaphysical tradition and no one responded." Not being familiar with metaphysics other than that which Joel had taught me, I, too, had not realized how contradictory to most current metaphysics his statement had been. In his talk he had declared that thought was not a power. As metaphysics was traditionally based on the power and importance of thought, his statement was indeed revolutionary. He was saying that God is the only power, not thought, that thoughts can lead to the God experience, but thought of itself is not power.

Years later I recognized a pattern in Joel's visits and understood the reason for his annual sessions. Every year, Joel would give a class on the West Coast, often one in Chicago, and one in New York. He would purposely not return for a year. He didn't want his followers to depend on his consciousness to hold them up or for them to be able to lean on him personally. When Joel came to town and spoke, his students would indeed experience a higher level of consciousness. Bit by bit, during the year that followed, they would come down from the high consciousness they had experienced, but not as far down as they had been before. The next year Joel would return and the process would be repeated, always leaving his followers ahead of where they had previously been. He wanted them to find their answers in themselves and not depend on him or his presence to keep holding them up.

Looking back on the entries I made in my diary after the Amsterdam experience and during the New York classes,

I can see now the deepening of the Infinite Way message in my consciousness:

*If there is only one life, that life is not separated and ended; so there is no re-incarnation. All life always is now.*

*Although I do not know what IT is I know that it is, and there is nothing else but it, therefore, I too am it—I and my Father are one.*

*The suggestion or appearance of evil is not sin—our acceptance or judgment is the sin.*

*The ability to see man impersonally comes from within—*

*The ability to see life spiritually comes only from within; so the Kingdom of God is within you.*

*My GRACE is thy sufficiency in all things.*

*My Grace IS thy sufficiency in all things.*

*My Grace is THY sufficiency in all things.*

*My Grace is thy SUFFICIENCY in all things.*

*My Grace is thy sufficiency IN all things.*

*My Grace is thy sufficiency in ALL things.*

*My Grace is thy sufficiency in all THINGS.*

*If your security is based on someone's good will, or any circumstances beyond a spiritual control, then welcome any discord that will take you out of that situation.*

*You have demonstrated materiality for those who have turned to you—Mother, John, and others—don't be tempted to try to or expect to demonstrate for yourself.*

*When you sympathize you stab in the back.*

*I can't heal or change anything, because I would only be trying to change my concept of that thing and I am where that concept exists, am part of it, so no part of the dream has power to change the dream—both illusions.*

*The self is crucified when there is nothing left to pray for.*

*I am the funnel. God is the large end; personal sense is the small end where the fruits appear.*

*God becomes man that we might become God.*

CHAPTER SEVEN

# The London Beginning

*W*hen I was preparing to go to London to help John with *The King and I,* Joel asked me to take a dozen copies of *The Infinite Way* with me to give t to Henry Thomas Hamblin, who lived in Chichester, an hour from London. Someone had sent Hamblin the book and it was so in line with his own beliefs that he contacted Joel and they began an intense correspondence. Similar to the monthly letter Joel sent to his mail list, Hamblin published England's most successful metaphysical magazine, *Science of Thought Review.*

Upon my arrival in England, I made the train trip to Hamblin's headquarters where he met me at the Chichester station. I was immediately impressed by this distinguished gentleman with his gray goatee and professorial appearance. He could easily have been thought to be a don at an English college. We drove to his office and cottage surrounded by a picture-book English rose garden, and where I met his welcoming staff and began a relationship which continues today, though Hamblin has long since departed.

Once again, Spirit had worked in an amazing way. If an American publisher doesn't make arrangements for a publication in a foreign country within a certain length of time, and a dozen copies of a book have been sent to that country by the author, it frees him to allow whomever he wants to publish the book there. Joel's original publisher, the Willing Press, was a small California publisher that was mainly designed to publish author-financed books such as Joel's and had very limited distribution. Because Joel's guidance had told him to have me take the books to England with me, it became possible for him to be published by Allen & Unwin, England's most important publisher of metaphysical books with worldwide distribution throughout the entire English-speaking world.

When Joel came to New York in the fall of 1953, he informed me that his inner instructions had told him to give the class and afterwards to go to England. At the conclusion of the class he stayed on for a while in New York and when I asked him his departure date for England, he said that he hadn't "gotten my orders" yet, meaning that until his inner voice gave him instructions he would stay put.

A few days later I got a cable from the most important actor's agent in London asking me if I would be interested in an actress named Dorothy Tutin to play the lead in a pro-posed London production of *I Am A Camera*. Dorothy had received rave notices for *The Living Room*, a Graham Greene play; however, she had become ill during the run and they had to close the production.

Despite the fact that she was still in the hospital, the agent asked me to come immediately if I was open to the possibility. I called Joel to tell him I was leaving for England as soon as possible, but before I could say anything he informed me that he had received his "orders" telling him to leave the next day. Talk about divine synchronicity! We booked the same flight and off we went on Joel's first London trip during his spiritual career.

The plane was an old-fashioned propeller plane. In those days we flew to Newfoundland, fueled up, hopped over to Shannon Airfield in Ireland to refuel again, and made the final leg to London. When we arrived over London the whole area was hidden beneath a blanket of clouds, and planes were unable to land. We circled the city a number of times, and finally the pilot announced that he had just enough fuel to make one more try. If we couldn't land, we would have to divert and land in Munich, Germany for the night. Joel looked over at me, and wrinkled his nose as if to say, "Is that so?" He punched the button to lay his seat back, closed his eyes, and began to meditate. Well, it was like the parting of the Dead Sea! A break appeared in the clouds and we landed. We were the only plane to get in that afternoon. The response I got from Joel was a smile and a wink.

Joel checked into the Washington Mayfair Hotel on Curzon Street and I into the Ritz a few blocks away. The next morning I called Joel and he asked me to come to his room. When I arrived the shades were drawn and the room was eerily dark. Joel was lying in bed in his pajamas. Though he didn't describe the symptoms, he told me that he wasn't feeling well and asked me to sit with him for a while. I had never seen him this vulnerable before, and I remember feeling that I was invading his privacy. Feeling highly inadequate, I tried to recall all Joel had taught me about healings and the necessity for one to experience the spiritual presence in order to affect a healing, but I felt helpless and unworthy. What could I do to heal this powerhouse of a man? After half an hour, mostly of silence, I left wondering if I had let him down, but a short time later Joel was up and about.

The next day I went to the hospital to meet the young actress, Dorothy Tutin, and immediately knew that she was the one I wanted to cast in the play. When I returned to my room I meditated and received an inner assurance that her health would not be a problem. The play opened a few months later and ran for over a year without Dorothy missing a single performance. In the meantime Joel visited Thomas Hamblin for the first time, contacted some local Christian Scientists, and met with the Unity minister. A date was chosen for Joel to return in a few months to lecture and give a class.

As it happened, not by accident I am sure, when the time came for Joel to return to London, divine synchronicity was still at work. A theater became available in London for my play and I arrived for rehearsals at the same time as Joel's class. He asked me to introduce him on his first public talk, which took place at Caxton Hall, and to assist in the class that followed.

In all of Joel's classes and lectures that I had been a part of, he had always been strictly impersonal and only made passing references to his past life and spiritual evolution. As far as I knew, and I knew him better and attended more of his lectures than anyone else, he had never opened himself up as personally to an audience as he did during that first London talk. So I was both surprised and fascinated when, before this formidable British audience, he started right by talking about himself and spent the first hour explaining how he had arrived at his beliefs.

As the audience was unfamiliar with his teaching, instead of jumping right into his mysticism, he offered them a necessary bridge from a personal sense. At the end of the class, Joel returned to Hawaii and I stayed on for rest of rehearsals and the opening of my play.

Eileen Bowden from Victoria, British Columbia, was visiting her daughter in London at the time of Joel's class. Of all his students, Eileen was Joel's favorite and, indeed, she was a remarkable light. Her smile could melt the hardest heart. She spoke softly and with humor, but there was always a twinkle in her eye and tremendous strength behind her words. I always felt that Joel would have asked Eileen to be his wife except for the fact that she was happily married.

The day after Joel left London, Eileen and I were going somewhere in a taxi when the conversation turned to Joel. I was still putting Joel on a pedestal in those days and took everything he said at face value. Before he left London, Joel had complained about being alone since his separation from Nadea, and I was feeling sorry for him. Eileen laughed and surprised me by her candor. In that moment she showed me that she saw the human in Joel without losing sight of his divine mission. She said, "Don't kid yourself. Joel can have all the companionship he wants whenever he really wants it."

After the class a number of those who had attended decided to form a group to study Joel's work; so before he left he asked Eileen to conduct the meetings as long as she was in London and for me to continue after she left. The group included a man named Walter Eastman, who continued to organize study groups and be the number one spokesman for Joel's work in England for years to come. With about 30 people in attendance, we met in a room above a health food store off Hyde Park Corner. Eileen would conduct a meditation and I would play a tape recording of one of Joel's talks.

After Eileen left the country it was up to me to carry on. In those days everything that was mailed to England had to go through a customs inspection, which often took quite a while. The tapes of the lectures Joel had sent from headquarters in Hawaii had not cleared customs in time for my first meeting; so I had to take the place of the tape recorder and speak to the group on my own.

Though I knew that I should depend on the Spirit to tell me what to say in my presentation, I made extensive notes, which I thought included enough material for an hour-long talk. At the meeting I was faced with a group of frozen English faces staring at me with a challenging look that said, "What's this young American theatrical producer going to have to say to us." My hour-long notes lasted about ten minutes and, though my lips were moving, inside myself I was frantically calling on help from God. Just in time my intuition, my inner tuition, kicked in and I began to hear what I was to say. That was the beginning of my lecturing history. Since that date, I never pre-plan what I am going to say in a talk other than my deciding on a general direction and an idea or two. Just like Joel, I have always known that unless my inner voice does the speaking, Walter won't have anything to talk about and he will be in trouble.

# 1954–1957

ℰarly the following year, 1954, Joel sent Frances Steloff the manuscript of *Living the Infinite Way*. She passed it along to Eugene Exman, who had built Harper & Row's religious department into the most respected religious publisher in America. After taking a look at Joel's manuscript, Exman called up Frances and said, "Is there someone close to Mr. Goldsmith that I could talk to about this manuscript?" Francis said, "Yes, Walter Starcke." Exman arranged for me to meet him at the Harvard Club for lunch and began by saying, "Mr. Goldsmith's book is repetitive, has no direct line, and needs a lot of work. How much will he do to re-write it?" I said, "Forget it! That's Joel's style and the repetition in the book is both on purpose and necessary. You either publish it as it is or let it go." He looked me in the eye for a time, nodded his head, and said, "Alright, I'll do it." Harper & Row not only published that book but also followed it by publishing all of Joel's other books until after his passing. Its successor, Harper Collins, still has a number of Joel's books in print 42 years after his death.

# The Monastic Impossibility

During this mid-fifties, period Joel jotted down brief messages that he received in his early morning meditations. From time to time he sent me the statements a few at a time as they came to him, written on flowery, half-sheet Hawaiian stationery. Later he combined them, called them the "Wisdoms," and added them to the end of *The Infinite Way*.

Joel sent me a wisdom that he called *The Monastic Life* which he said could only be given to advanced students because it could be harmful for those not ready for it. However, later it was included in the 1956 letters, Chapter 17. Its absolutism put another nail in the coffin of my attempt to kill personal sense.

He wrote that in order to live the monastic life we should be cut off from all emotional attachments, "knowing no deep devotion to any person or thing." He added that in the monastic life there is "no deep love for any individual, nor is there a need for mother, brother, wife, or friend." He said that it could be lived in the world without emotional interchange in human relationships because emotions are a drain depleting the spiritual power inherent in the true monastic life.

Joel might have been talking about the goal he set for himself, when he admitted that those called to the monastic life may have the remaining hidden longing for "closer companionship with those of his family or friends or religious circle—even sometimes a deep desire for home—but he has not the capacity to enjoy or remain in them." He said that these human desires are often leaks in the insulation or a leftover from the last human experience on earth.

The "Wisdom's" absolute advice extended to "It is this inability to fuse that makes the mystic difficult to live with or work with. Always, the spiritual light serves as a barrier to emotional reaction—and for the sake of his friends and relatives it would be better for those living the monastic life to separate themselves from personal contacts. Then the impersonal life of love is lived without strain or drain upon one's resources of spiritual power."

Believing in Joel absolutely and believing that absolutes were possible to live at the personal level, I dedicated myself completely to living them with heart and soul. As a successful and not unattractive Broadway producer in my mid-thirties, from 1954 to 1957 every temptation was thrown at me, all to no avail. I didn't drink or smoke and I put all thoughts of sex totally out of my mind.

I tried to be as absolutely impersonal as I could be in all my actions, business or interpersonal. I was operating under the belief that I could or should completely deny my humanity. I was going to storm the spiritual gates and become an enlightened soul no matter how insensitive to human feeling I would be. Eventually I became a little monster! Apart from an impersonal compassion for all human kind, by trying to separate myself from personal sense, I was cutting myself off from my own feelings. I could see someone run over by a taxi or starving children in Africa and feel nothing under the guise of claiming that appearances were illusion.

Every time the phone rang I would affirm that God was the only power by saying to myself, "Thank you Father," and then I would answer the call. I dealt strictly with impersonal principle. If an actor in a play that I was producing warranted the salary of somewhere between $400 and $500 a week, I would negotiate within that range but wouldn't pay less than $400 even though the actor would pay me to be in the play if it came down to that. I wouldn't pay more than 500, because I would tell myself that God was all I needed and that no human being was indispensable.

In my belief that personal sense was my enemy, I was running away from my human identity and becoming unfeeling and insensitive. Nevertheless, during the next three years I filled several diaries with the spiritual "clicks" I had experienced and the quotes that made an impact on me. Here are a few of the entries:

> *God is the son of God.*
> *The truth I seek I am.*

> *Huxley: "Few are chosen—for few choose themselves."*

> *Eckhart: "A man should be as free of his own knowledge as when he did not exist. So poor there is no place for God to work. I pray God to rid me of God because conditionless being is above God and above distinction. It was in this that I became myself. I willed myself and know myself*

*to make this man called "I" and I am my own cause. For this am I born. My birth is eternal and can never die. What I am in time will die. In my birth all things were born, if I had not been born then God would not have been either."*

*Judas will betray, Peter will deny, Thomas will doubt—BUT IT MAKES NO DIFFERENCE— we expect nothing of Thomas—all we expect is of God.*

Obsessed with the belief that everything should have spiritual content, I encouraged van Druten to write a play that would include principles of *The Infinite Way*. He wrote one called *I've Got Sixpence*, about two young people's spiritual search and the influence of a Joel-type master.

We tried to get Marlon Brando to play the young male lead. John had given Brando his first Broadway part in his play *I Remember Mama,* and Brando had great respect for John. He read the new play and agreed to star in it. The circumstances that followed taught me several valuable lessons.

Believing that Brando was going to be in the play even though he never returned to Broadway following his appearance in *A Streetcar Named Desire* in 1947, I rushed ahead and signed for a particular theater that I wanted before I had Brando's name on the dotted line. He stalled and stalled until it became obvious that he would never sign and, as I had committed us to a theater, John and I had to compromise and get the best actor for the part that we could. Unfortunately, the one we settled on wasn't up to the part, and that contributed significantly to the play's demise—that was lesson #1.

Lesson #2: The play was too much of a polemic. We were trying to preach Infinite Way principles rather than reveal the consciousness of them through the drama, so the play had no internal energy. In *Bell, Book and Candle,* we had cloaked the message in a comedy plot, letting the story convey the message without preaching, and the play was alive. This time intellect swallowed the principle of good theater. In trying to institutionalize our beliefs by preaching, we were making the same mistake theologians have always made. The theater, or the church, should be used to create the experience of a desired state of consciousness and not just talk about it.

From this painful mistake I learned what it means to live in the "now." It doesn't mean that one should not plan for the future. It is just that there is a "now" for making decisions that will affect the future. For instance, there is a right "now" for a producer to lease a theater though he wouldn't be occupying the theater until months later. The proper time to sign contracts is after several necessary elements are in place.

After a play has been optioned by a producer, the next step is for the producer to hire the right director, after which the producer, author, and director together each have a veto on the cast. Before going further they should get the star under contract before leasing a theater, which I didn't do.

For the steps in a production to make sense, a producer and author seek a director who understands and appreciates the values in the play in the same way they do, and one who is fired up about doing it. Then the producer, author, and director agree upon a star that they all believe is the best possible one for the part. After those elements are in place it is safe to sign a contract for a theater.

# Letters to John and Me

*I*n the summer of 1955, John and I rented my co-producer Gert's home at Sneeden's Landing on the Hudson River a few miles north of the George Washington Bridge. Gert had a cottage on Martha's Vineyard where she summered. I would commute to my office on 52nd Street daily while preparing for a fall production in New York. During this period our correspondences with Joel continued. There was a difference in the way Joel would speak to John and to me. He would speak to John more as an equal, at far greater length, from a more intellectual than mystical approach, and to John he would say some things that he would not say in public. His letters to me were shorter and more teacher to student.

In the following extensive letter, Joel makes comments on Jesus and the Essenes that will shock some people even today. The article Joel refers to in the letter is one that John sent him about the Essenes and the *Dead Sea Scrolls* that was published in the New Yorker magazine.

On June 6, 1955 Joel wrote that it would be his joy to visit us and spend a couple of days in our home on the Hudson. He then went into a lengthy discussion on the use of mantras, saying that his use of them was different than the Hindu. He said that when a Bible quote such as "Thy Grace is my sufficiency in all things" came to him, it would repeat itself many times a day, perhaps for days. Finally the statement would register in his subconscious and would surface when needed. He said he might give the quote to someone for immediate use, but he would not teach it as a necessity.

He said that in the same fashion, John should realize that his repeated use of Luke 12, 22 - 32 was based on the fact that early in his spiritual life the "Take no thought" technique had made itself so clear to him that it virtually became a mantra, "And for quite some time whenever there was a suggestion of lack of anything or any activity, immediately this statement would return to my consciousness: that I was to take no thought for the things of this life." He said that finally the principle became his consciousness and he would use it only in teaching or to give it to someone as a temporary mantram.

Joel then went into a lengthy discourse about how every inharmony or discord was based only on the belief in separation from God, and that it became virtually a mantram with him, so that at every appearance of discord, in himself or others, he would return immediately to the conscious realization that there is no claim present except the sense of separation from Source.

Joel went into even greater detail about an article that appeared in the New Yorker that he thought was "fascinating and illuminating." He said that there was nothing in the article that he had not known, but that he had gotten it through inner revelation and hadn't seen it in print before. He then went on to say something that I expect he meant only for John's ears.

Joel wrote that despite Jesus' experiences with the Essenes he was not the greatest; rather it was John, of the Gospel of John, who went a lot further than Jesus. He said, "Christ Jesus was only an actor in the drama of His period, and undoubtedly lived out the career as Great Master of the Order, succeeding the original righteous Teacher."

Joel claimed that when the Master was crucified, only a few in Jerusalem had any awareness of it except those of the

Sanhedrin who were responsible. He said that the multitudes to whom Jesus preached and whom he healed were not there;rather that was fantasy built up 300 years later by the church.

Joel wrote, "All of these things I learned on the Inner plane, and many more besides." He doubted that anyone could understand unless they also heard it on the Inner plane, or after the manuscripts that the article talked of were translated in their fullness and ultimately published. When that happened, he said it could be "the beginning of the end of Christianity as we know it today."

Joel proceeded to give a lengthy dissertation on the importance of a movement like the Essenes, in that it develops the ability to teach from the Inner plane. He wrote that most likely of the thousands who were Essenes, only a few attained mastership to the extent of receiving the ability to receive and impart teaching via the Inner plane. Such masters never die but merely pass behind the scene so that they may there better carry on the work of spiritual impartation. He lamented the end of the Essene establishment in 68 A.D. and might have been referring to the Infinite Way when he said, "It is for this reason that there is a need today for just such an organization so that this ability to commune and communicate on the Inner plane could be once more taught."

Joel added that "when one finds a student of sufficiently developed consciousness, it is possible to work in and through their consciousness as their own consciousness, so that there is not the natural rebellion that arises in receiving impartations from a teacher on the human plane." He explained that the impartations came as an activity of the student's own consciousness and there would be no need to acknowledge or be second to the teacher.

Joel added that this was the reason he no longer took

on students for the higher teaching, because he found it better to get his message across to those whom he could reach on the Inner plane. In this way he was as much behind the scene as if he actually passed from human experience. He ended the letter with love to John and me.

At Joel's suggestion, when I was in Los Angeles in 1956, I helped a student of Joel's named Ruth set up an Infinite Way reading room. Encouraging me, Joel wrote the following letter, a letter that shows how differently he talked to me than to John.

After the salutation he said, "Your letter of Thursday afternoon is amazing and I am deeply grateful." He shared it with Emma and Floyd and was happy that my powers of discernment were alive. He said that as he had worked with me—never pushing or even encouraging me—he had let me be moved by spirit. He told me to discourage public work rather than encourage it and wait for guidance to push me into action. As a warning he said for me to never be tempted to forget that he had been spiritually guided every step of the Infinite Way, that it was God's activity and that God alone was responsible for it. He said that I couldn't realize this unless I looked back to the time when we first met and recognized how God had made every move, and that even the mistakes made were necessary for this experience. Ever teaching, he added, "Keep your periods of meditation plentiful, but short, and accept my God guidance."

Prophetically, in this letter he said he was grateful to Ruth for having started his first reading room in Los Angeles and for her work, and that he would stop off in Los Angeles on his way to Chicago to see the Reading Room and meet with us.

Within six months Joel wrote me two letters that showed he wasn't beyond having a learning experience himself that year. Although he had always said that he would not be tempted to form an organization or appoint official teachers, when he allowed Ruth to open a reading room in Los Angeles similar to those that were popular in the Christian Science organization, it didn't take long for him to regret going back on his own guidance.

Excerpts from his next letter showed the crack that was beginning to appear in Joel's relationship with Ruth. He wrote, "Am having my hands full with her. Ego is riding wild—and riding for a fall." He said that her letters had been irrational, saying that she was going to leave her home and be with him, sitting at the feet of the master. In her letter to Joel she had said that she didn't care whether her husband and son hated her, and Joel added, "You can imagine my answers—or can you really?"

The final letter to me on the subject of Ruth was written January 30, 1957, not too many months before a disturbing change in Joel's and my relationship was about to occur. He started by thanking me for my "fine letter" and that I would see the righteousness of my work become tangibly evident. He said that my progress was certain because of my "spiritual integrity." He once more repeated that Ruth was "bad medicine," and that she had given a talk on "sex, dope, and alcohol as perversions," as well as her saying that meditations were not real unless you tingled and had out-of-this-world experiences. After a few more complaints about Ruth, he ended the letter telling me to come home whenever I was ready and that "the lamp is always hanging in the window."

CHAPTER EIGHT

# The Breakup

*P*rophecy wouldn't be prophetic if we could hear or believe it before the fact. Despite my having read and re-read these quotes that followed each other in Joel's "Wisdoms," it took until the next few years for them to prove themselves in my life:

> *When the spiritual student's house of cards crumbles, he is near to "a house not made with hands, eternal in the heavens."*

> *Spiritual Students! Rejoice as the outer building tumbles down, for the inner Temple is to be revealed.*

> *To those unfolding on the spiritual path, come the discordant experiences of human life, until the transition from "this world" has been completely accomplished. The desire is to avoid or escape those inharmonies of mind, body, or economic affairs—but this cannot be done, since the discords result solely from the battle*

*with Spirit and "the flesh," that is, with spiritual consciousness and material sense.*

*When your spiritual study is sincere, the breaking up of your material world—the desertion of friends, students, or family, a change of health or other outer activity—often ushers in the spiritual transition, or rebirth. This is the attainment of that which you have sought.*

After twelve years of perfect harmony and understanding between Joel and me, there was no way I could have believed that in a year our relationship would change and seem to deteriorate. Nor could I ever have believed that what I thought was my failure would turn out to be my success. A variety of dramatic and life-altering events took place in 1956 and 1957 that ultimately affected Joel's, John's, and my lives in dramatic and life-altering ways.

It all began when I was visiting John at his ranch. I had fixed up the little parlor in the guest wing as a kind of sanctuary where I would meditate when at the ranch. I made a little altar on the coffee table, covered it with a gold cloth on which I had an OUM symbol stitched in gold sequins. The altar was strewn with fresh flowers that I would pick every morning, and at the center I placed a composite picture of holy men that included Ramakrishna, Jesus, Buddha, Joel, and others. Incense and a lighted candle completed the picture. I sat on the floor cross legged before the altar to meditate for up to a couple of hours every morning, sometimes being called away to help John on a project in his office.

One day John asked me if he could join me for my meditations, and of course I agreed. Rather than sitting on the floor, he sat in a chair behind me, and we began.

We meditated together for several days, and on the second day he excitedly told me that he had had the "click," the identifiable experience of the Spirit that everyone strives for. Despite the fact that John had meditated with Joel and Swami Prabhavananda many times, he claimed this was the first time that he had actually experienced a recognizable inner contact. That night, to my surprise and not aware of its full significance, I wrote in my diary, "Your purpose in John's life is over!"

That meditation experience took place shortly after John's 54th birthday. When I revisited those years, I realized it was then that John's life started to fall to pieces. John wrote another play while I was in New York, and when I arrived at his ranch to help with the rewrites I was shocked by what I read. The play lacked energy and was like a parody of his usual scintillating style. It was as though his creative light had gone out. I knew if I told him that the play had no life in it, and that I thought it would not succeed, he would put it away and no one would ever see it again. I didn't want that responsibility; so I made him promise me that before I told him what I thought of the play he would send a copy to Christopher Isherwood and the playwright Dodie Smith and ask their opinions. He did, and they wrote back with the same judgment as mine, and the play was then put aside.

Later in the year John wrote another play, *Dancing in the Chequred Shade,* about a triangle between a young actress, her *Catcher in the Rye*-like Harvard dropout boyfriend, and an eccentric James Dean-type movie actor. I read the play and saw immediately that, like the previous one, it was not up to John's usual standard.

By this time I was seriously concerned about John's state of mind and the doldrums he seemed to be stuck in since his previous aborted effort. In thirty years of success he had never had an unproduced play before, and I felt that though this new one was not up to Hoyle, it would be too much for him to have another rejection right on top of the other one.

I talked to John about the play's problems, meditated long and hard, made some suggestions for a rewrite, and once again left New York for the ranch to help. I was so convinced that the play was risky that before going into production I raised enough money to close the show on the road if necessary, fix any mistakes, re-rehearse, and re-open.

John and I decided to see if James Dean would be interested in playing the part we had modeled after him. An appointment was set up for us to meet with him at Warner Brothers Studio. Dean was shooting *Giant* at the time and had come to the studio to do some dubbing (changes in the original sound track) for *Rebel Without a Cause*. John and I watched the performance, which was really no more than a series of re-recorded grunts and groans, and then we met with Dean. The defensive and disturbed energy he projected on the screen was clearly his personal consciousness. He entered the room like a trapped animal, suspicious and restless. Instead of offering John the respect he was usually accorded, Dean seemed about to attack, and I had to intercede. After a brief explanation, I gave Dean the manuscript and we exited. With Dean's self-destructive consciousness it wasn't hard to predict his future, as we left the studio I heard myself say, "He is going to die, violently and before very long." A week later my prophecy came true; James Dean died in a car crash, reportedly with our manuscript in his car.

After we returned to New York to complete casting and other pre-production details, John received two soul-shaking blows. The Saddler's Wells Ballet Company, later the Royal Ballet, was giving its first live American television performance of *The Nutcracker Suite* on NBC. John was asked to write a script clarifying the plot and setting the stage for those unfamiliar with the ballet. He wrote a charming script that was to be played before the performance about two parents explaining the ballet to their children, during act breaks, and after the performance. The newspapers made a big deal about how much John was being paid for the few minutes of dialogue.

On the night of the show John and I went to see the televised performance in a viewing room at NBC. The live performance ran longer than expected; so without consulting with John they cut his script to the point that it made no sense. As a result the reviewers tore John to pieces for having received so much money for what they called gibberish. John, never one to show his rage or hurt feelings, internalized his anguish and said little. It would have been much better for him if he had exploded and let it out.

The second blast, and a much more personal and confusing one, came via a letter from Joel, who was then in London. John, at my encouragement, had finished writing an autobiographical book, *The Way To The Future*, that he had begun many years before but put aside. It covered his life up until the time he became successful at age 24, and it had just come out in America and England. Joel had picked up a copy at a book store in London. He read it and immediately sat down and wrote John the most scathing letter imaginable. Joel said the book was filthy and that John should stop publication immediately and buy up all the copies that were in print.

I was confused at Joel's response because I felt that the book couldn't have been more innocent, and I was surprised when later Joel pointed out what had upset him. John had mentioned that during his teen years he had wondered what it took place when his mother and father were in bed. Joel said that was a filthy thought and not worthy of anyone connected with the Infinite Way. As far as I could see, that was the only reference John made to anything even remotely off-color in the whole book. I felt that there had to be some other reason behind Joel's response.

Coming right on top of the televised ballet debacle, Joel's reaction to the book crushed John. I knew Joel was God-guided and that he wasn't just being malicious. I begged John not to look at the situation at face value. I told him that there had to be some hidden lesson behind Joel's action, even if Joel himself was not consciously aware of what it was.

Later I came to the conclusion that without his even knowing it, Joel was trying to save John's life. It wasn't that Joel had psychologically figured out the identity crisis John was going through and was trying to jolt him into rediscovering himself; it was just that Joel followed his own guidance impeccably and did what it said for him to do, often without knowing why. However, John responded in the one way he shouldn't have. Instead of taking responsibility for his life and affirming his own spiritual identity by telling Joel to mind his own business, or completely submitting himself to his guru's consciousness, John just sulked and did nothing. He neither sought help from his own spiritual source or help from anyone else.

A week after completing the casting of the new play, *Dancing in the Chequred Shade*, we started rehearsals. After a few days I became concerned. John had always directed his own plays but he wasn't taking hold as he had in the past. Never had I felt the need to overcome such a strong negative pull. I meditated as much as I could to clear the air; however, after several nights of terrible nightmares and intense nocturnal dreams, I felt shaken, spiritually drained, and unable to make my inner contact. It was as though a hand came down on us determined to throw every possible obstacle in our way, and a series of unfortunate events began to happen. It was clear that we were heading toward a crisis.

When we were casting the play a young man absolutely captivated us by his audition for one of the two leading men's parts. John had given Marlon Brando his first part in a Broadway play, *I Remember Mama*, and Sir Laurence Olivier his first leading role in a West End play in London; so believing he was making another important discovery, we cast the actor. During rehearsals the young man was so brilliant that we felt he would carry the play no matter what weaknesses the script had. It made no sense, but as soon as we started giving previews before an audience, the actor seemed to resent the audience's presence, and he systematically destroyed his performance. Perhaps he missed the privacy of his acting class where there wasn't any audience to intrude, but bit by bit in each of the following performances, the actor killed all the places where the audience would have responded, and we couldn't stop him.

The other male lead in the play was the part we had wanted James Dean to play, a sympathetic yet unsympathetic character. But the actor we had cast just turned out to be unsympathetic, period; so we replaced him with his understudy, George Maharis, who later starred in the television series, *Route 66*. On opening night in Boston with the critics present, Maharis panicked, broke into a sweat, could hardly get his lines out, and ran out of the theater at the end of the play without taking any curtain calls. It was the single most humiliating night I had ever spent. I couldn't replace him with the understudy because he was the understudy.

Here are two entries I made in my diary, one a few days before I closed the show and the other after. At that time, I was still living the complete monastic life and attempting to tell myself I was above human concerns:

> *For a week things have gotten steadily worse. Whenever a thread of hope appears I clutch at it. Yesterday not even a thread remained and I faced the fact that it was hopeless. My grief is deep because I can't see how I can stand up and say 'Live as I live' when everything I do fails. I don't just want to demonstrate 'for' myself, but I've followed what I felt was my guidance and principle and find it doesn't work. Maybe I was relying on truth or principle as a formula I could follow for results. I still hope Joel can personally help. (Just got a cable from Joel saying 'I have not left you.') Without a conscious realization of God how can I live and—There is just nothing I can do.*

An agonizing week later, having closed the show, I wrote the following entry:

> *Still the blackest nightmare. Things steadily worse. Lots of tears when I think of God. No sense to life. The worse thing is that I can no longer believe in my "voices" and "revelations." I don't want to return to old habits yet I must have God. Every time I meditate I get hit again, but still I want God more than anything—More than life itself. Oh Hell.*

As the producer I had to endure and deal with the agony of all that goes with a closing. Before a show opens all the suppliers are sweetness and light, but if the show gets bad notices they swarm around like vultures, afraid they will not get paid. John returned to his ranch in California to rewrite the play. I stayed on to put the set in storage and deal with my own depression. By the time I was finished I wanted nothing more than to escape to Hawaii to spend time with Joel and lick my wounds.

I wrote Joel that I wanted to visit him, and I was totally crushed when he wrote back telling me not to come, saying that he had no more to teach me at the moment. I knew how far I had yet to go and felt lost. So I meditated and sent him a cable saying, "I don't want you to teach me any more. I want your consciousness itself." Joel immediately cabled back, "Swell, come ahead."

Joel had bought a little house on the beach in Kailua, across the Pali Pass from Honolulu on the windward side of Oahu. When I arrived he took me into the spare bedroom he had converted into his office, and I began to unload my frustration and bellyache about my life and the demise of the show. All of a sudden Joel held up his hand to stop me, and in substance said, "I can't talk to a sick mind. Just hang around, walk on the beach, read, or watch television, and we will go to dinner. In time we will talk again when you are back to yourself."

We went to dinner that night at a little Japanese steak house around the corner. The next morning when I arrived, Joel was answering mail as usual. I settled in to his big green leather chair in the living room, the kind that has a foot rest that comes up when you lie back. At this point I was still in the doldrums feeling more emotionally numb than anything else. All of a sudden, for some unknown reason, it was like a plug being pulled and I began to cry. Tears flooded down my face. For a couple of minutes I was a blubbering mess. When I pulled out of it and dried my face, Joel came to the door and motioned for me to come into his office.

When I sat down Joel asked, "Now what's the problem?" I looked at him, took stock, shook my head, smiled sheepishly, and said, "Nothing. I feel like I just woke up from a nightmare. I don't know why I was so upset. So what, the play failed. It's not the end of the world." All the darkness had just vanished. Nothing had changed, but the light was shining again, and I was as happy as could be. I was amazed at how miserable I had been such a short a time ago. Once and for all, I saw what tricks the mind can play on us, how it hypnotizes us, and the lesson I learned was worth the pain. I also felt that just being in Joel's vibration broke the illusion.

The show's failure might have been a big price to pay for what I learned, but never again, even in the depths of a dark night experience that happened years later, did I forget that every sense of separation from God, and all fear, is created by the thinking mind. Our minds create both our sense of good and of bad, and it is up to us to choose which to accept regardless of appearances. That didn't mean that from then on I could always easily snap out of it when things looked bad, but it helped me to remember "this too shall pass" and be a bit more patient until the condition would break and I would no longer be deceived by my mind.

During the next week or so I hung around during the daytime and listen to Joel dictate his often cryptic letters. Every night Floyd Nowell would join us and we would talk a while, meditate, break for a cup of coffee, then meditate a while more.

Emma now lived a few blocks away from Joel. She had left her job at the beauty parlor, had set up a tape duplicating operation in her garage, and worked for Joel full-time. She would come and go to Joel's house during the day, would keep the refrigerator stocked, and made herself generally indispensable. Emma was always unobtrusive, quiet, and a pleasant presence. She wouldn't join us in meditation but would hover around supplying us with coffee and diet-denying sweet pastries on our breaks.

Those meditations with Joel and Floyd are among the most cherished memories of my life. One time Joel was lying back in his big green chair and began to snore during our meditation. I said, "Joel, you went to sleep." He scowled at me and denied that he had. Floyd was the one person who could kid Joel and bring him to task at times, and always with a sense of humor that made his remarks harmless. Those were great times. I never felt so content, free, and fulfilled. It was as though I were drinking the nectar of life.

## *John's Crisis*

*M*eanwhile, things were not going so well for our friend, John van Druten. For the rest of the year, after I closed *Dancing in the Chequred Shade* in Boston, there was no letup for him. It hurt to see this sensitive grand man be hit over and over with adversity. He returned to his ranch and rewrote the failed play, six short stories, a 60,000-word book, and finally a movie script, all in six months. The movie script was the straw that broke the proverbial camel's back.

Burt Lancaster's production company commissioned John to write a movie based on Ivan S. Turgenev's short story *First Love*. John was then in residence at his apartment in Hollywood and went to the producer's office every morning for story conferences. As John would improvise, the producers would rave over his ideas, and would laugh at his humorous lines. What they didn't know was that John had a great memory for dialogue and was writing the play in his head during these story sessions. When he actually sat before the typewriter to write the manuscript, he finished it in five days.

John was being paid $125 thousand for a script containing less than two hours of dialogue, which is the equivalent of a million dollars today. I arrived in Hollywood just as he finished the manuscript and said, "John, their egos can't take paying you that enormous amount of money for what they will see as only five days work. Let's go over to Hawaii, visit Joel for a couple weeks, and on your return their egos won't balk when you submit the script." John refused my advice, and something within me told me that destiny was at work, that I was to stay out of the process, and not try to insist. He handed the script over that day.

The very next day Lancaster's people called John and referred to the script with a dirty word, said there wasn't a shootable line in it, and that they were not going to pay him. John was so highly respected that I doubt anyone had ever been so rude to him before. This time, instead of sulking in private, he did something I was proud of him for doing. He turned the situation over to the Screenwriter's Guild. They had never before had an author of John's stature put a project of this kind in their hands for resolution.

The actual court case wasn't to take place until some time later. John had to stay on in California for depositions and I went to Chicago with Joel to work on a class he was to give there. John was to follow after his union meetings were over.

Near the end of the class in Chicago, John arrived from California and something happened that told me that what he had been going through was taking a toll on him. Joel, John, and I were walking down the boulevard in front of the Statler Hotel when John suddenly stopped and said he was having a difficult time walking. Joel closed his eyes for a second, and even though he had taught that we are not doctors and should not diagnose, he opened his eyes and said, "It's from indigestion. It will be all right." Nevertheless, we discontinued our walk and returned to our rooms. The next day Joel went back to Hawaii and John and I returned to New York.

A day later John called me from the Dorset Hotel and said that he couldn't get out of bed. I immediately dressed and went to his hotel, took one look at him, and called an ambulance. Though John was only 56 years old, he was experiencing heart failure. He had habitually ignored his body, exercised very little, and routinely ate rich gourmet meals.

On one of my visits to the hospital, I was handling my concern with confident assurance that everything would be all right until something startling happened that let me know how deep my feelings for John went. When I arrived I was informed that there had been a mix-up in the reading of John's chart and two separate nurses had given him diuretic shots one on top of the other resulting in his having a heart attack. I almost fainted when I heard the news and had to sit down with my head between my knees.

In time John was well enough to leave the hospital. He returned to the Dorset Hotel and I would go over from my hotel to fix him salt-free meals in the butler's pantry of his suite. Before long I saw that John was not quite himself. He didn't respond to our interchanges as he had in the past, and his usual humor was missing. He didn't want to meditate. At times I almost felt like a stranger. The doctors told me that he would be ready to travel after a couple of weeks. My job was to nurse him back to strength.

When Carter, who ran John's ranch in California and managed his business affairs, came to the hospital, I urged him to let me take John to Palm Beach or some other warm place and get him back in shape before he returned to the ranch. I felt that if John went straight back home he would continue his usual routine, get on the typewriter, and kill himself trying to maintain his old purpose for living.

Carter seemed to agree with me, but on his return to California he hired John's butler and cook to come to the ranch two months earlier than their usual time knowing that John would insist on returning if he knew they were there. Once more, I didn't try to interfere, and John went back to his ranch. He immediately resumed his old routine. Shortly, he wrote a stage adaptation of *The Anatomy of a Murder*, hardly the kind of subject that his love-filled plays were usually about, and he died the day after he finished it.

John literally committed suicide on the typewriter. He had been successful since he was 24 years old and he couldn't imagine an identity other than that of a successful playwright. From this experience I learned two things.

John had come into this incarnation at the stage of his spiritual evolution where he was to intellectually work with the letter of truth until he arrived at an actual spiritual experience of his own higher consciousness. Once that had been accomplished, he was ready to move from a mental approach to life to a life lived by mystical intuition. But John had been such a successful public figure for so many years that he couldn't reinvent himself. He had to shed his old identity in order to go on. I also learned that in a number of cases, after a heart attack people drastically change. Whereas in the past, they had somewhat of a spiritual sense of self, after their life threatening experience they see their own lives and others in a purely material sense of being. When that happens, subjective reasoning no longer takes place and a purely objective approach colors their decisions from then on.

Sometime later I was discussing John's situation with Tennessee Williams, who also knew and respected John. When I said that I felt John had done himself in on his typewriter after his light went out, Tennessee said, "After I was 54 I wasn't top dog any more and I tried to kill myself with drugs for the next ten years until I got so bored with being miserable that I just stopped." He also never wrote another successful play after he was in his early fifties.

# The Conflict

*1957* was a roller coaster year for me with more lows than highs. The end of John van Druten's too short life was the lowest point. Whereas I lost the love and companionship of one of my two father figures, that year marked the beginning of a dramatic and painful turning point in my relationship with the other, Joel, my spiritual father.

The change actually began at the Chicago class just before John's heart attack. Whether the difficulties of the past couple of years had pushed me into it or whether the lessons I had learned had served their purpose, during the class my seven year monastic period came to an end just as suddenly as it had begun, and my guidance told me to go back into the world exposing myself to all its temptations. After I experienced the lifting of my monastic intent, prophetically at that time I told some of my friends that I felt my whole life was now going to change. The result wasn't what I expected.

Whereas, the desire for sex, the accumulation of money, seeking public recognition, and having a "good time" are what motivates human nature, I could take them or leave them. I could eat a gourmet dinner or have a hamburger with equal relish. There was only one thing that I sought —experiencing the presence of God—and that is the most illusive goal possible. My problem was the reverse of over-indulgence. Sometimes I had to make myself go out, have a couple of drinks, and participate in some nightlife and such because I knew that, for me, the gap had to be closed between my divinity and my humanity, and that would not happen if I went to either extreme.

The first confusing breakdown in Joel's and my communications resulted because of a conference I attended at Chautauqua. An elderly lady named Lucy Milligan, who was a good friend of Eleanor Roosevelt, was on a number of important boards and committees and headed the Peabody Awards committee. She was a regular at my Goldsmith tape meetings at the Gotham Book Mart. Lucy asked me to participate in a conference for twenty leaders of the nation's top charities—heart, tuberculosis, cancer, etc.—on the subject of volunteer workers and how to encourage their participation.

When I arrived at Chautauqua for the conference and was shown to my room, I meditated and "it" said, "Speak when spoken to." Well, no one spoke to me! At least, no one asked my opinion about what was going on; so I had a frustrating time. Lucy sensed this, and on the last day she went around the circle asking everyone their opinions of the meeting. When it was my turn, I told them it was a failure, that

I felt they had things in reverse. They were concentrating on what the volunteers could do for them rather than on what volunteering could do for the volunteers. I said that everyone needs to give in order to have a fulfilled life and they were offering that opportunity. Well, everyone responded in a very positive way, which resulted in their unanimously suggesting that I write up the press release for both the United and Associated Press; so I wrote about the content of the meeting from its spiritual implications. When the releases went out I sent them to Joel with a cover note.

My turning the meeting around in a meaningful and offbeat way was similar to some experiences of Joel's that he had told me about; so I thought he would be pleased that his spiritual son had done the same. Instead, I got a letter back from him completely misinterpreting what I had written and implying that I had no right to speak up before such an august group. Frankly, I couldn't understand why. I wasn't bragging on myself. I gave spirit the credit, and I thought he would be proud of me.

Up until this time, in private Joel corrected me on spiritual matters and held up a high standard, but he never criticized my personal conduct or found fault with me or my actions. In public his approval of me implied that I could do no wrong. That is why his surprisingly demeaning response was the first sign that some unusual tension was beginning to build between us.

Joel made a quick trip to New York that spring and while there he seriously questioned me about my future plans in a way that he had not in the past. He implied that I was failing because I hadn't left the business world and dedicated myself to "the work." He gave me the feeling that he thought my elegant apartment with its 20-foot-high ceilings in the Des Artistes apartments looking out over rooftops onto the

Tavern on the Green in Central Park, was debauchery, as was the 100-year-old Conch House I had acquired in Key West, Florida. Whereas in the past Joel had made me feel that grace was directing my life now he made me feel I was personally responsible for my choices, which weren't all that spiritual.

After Joel returned to Hawaii I wrote him the following letter, which I now see set the stage in consciousness for what happened later that year, and its spiritually significant outcome.

*Dear Joel,*

*The other night you said something to the effect that I wouldn't speak up as to what I wanted to do; so I am sitting before this typewriter now in an attempt to speak up to myself as well as you.*

*The other day a friend said to me, "Starcke, you're immobile, because you don't have anything you want; or rather, you don't know what you want." It's true that human beings act because they have unfulfilled desires, and it is true that most of my human desires have been eliminated from my consciousness; however there has always been one very strong desire, and that is to attain the awareness of the presence of God, and the actual consciousness of the principles of the Infinite Way.*

*There is no doubt that I possess the equipment to attain any amount of worldly success and wealth if only the desire were within me to attain them—but I too well realize that there is no answer in occupation, activity, or companionship born of the dream, made of the substance of carnal mind; so the impetus that is needed for me to function at that level isn't operative.*

*Yet there is one activity that does at times take place in my life that leaves me with the sense of fulfillment, purpose, and joy. I do find that when I am placed in a group and the inner valve is opened, words pour forth and a process of "lifting" the group in consciousness takes place in a manner or level that I can only believe to be the Infinite Way consciousness. I know that at these moments I feel completely free of my personal sense of self, I am lifted, I am listening, and I feel "for this was I born."*

*Now, so far, this lifting of consciousness seems to take place with people who are not familiar with the Infinite Way and who would not perhaps make contact with it just by being handed a book or by hearing a tape—but after our sessions they are opened to the writings and the tapes, and often my function with them seems to change or have fulfilled itself—though I feel a bond and a strong sense of love from them that continues always.*

*I cannot help but feel that the real and unique blessing that has been given to me is the ability to "open" or ignite. Yet, these conclusions are not drawn from thought but from looking back at consciousness manifesting in form; so, by the same token, I look at the present form and see that I have manifested no full time activity or direction of a spiritual nature. I do know the inner voice well enough to know that any action other than that that is present would have been born by myself out of the fear of inactivity, or the turning to a recognized form out of fear that the one which repeats "for this was I born" will not come out of the invisible.*

*I also am well aware of one terrifying aspect—to attempt to speak, to attempt to lift other's consciousness, etc. without the spirit turning it on is a poisonous experience. I would rather die than go through that having known what it is to have the spirit speak through me. Yet, I also know that every year the voice gets closer to yours, closer to the I AM voice, and each year I am glad I didn't speak in public before the right time.*

*It seems there is no need at this very moment (though there may be tomorrow) for me to be doing whatever it is that I have been put in your life for. Yet there has been no one you have given more to, put more time in on, poured more of your soul into, than to me, and your life is too God-directed for you to have done this without its contributing to the fulfillment of the Infinite Way.*

*Finally, I think the greatest betrayal of you that I could perform would be for me to have, before this time, before the appointed time, left the world, hung out a sign or made an attempt to appear as Mr. Infinite Way Junior…Sure, it would have been easier and more comfortable than this not knowing what I am meant to do, and this living on the invisible, but I, of all people, must fulfill the Infinite Way—and the core of the Infinite Way is "demonstration."*

*As far as I know, these feelings are what I recognize. I can voice them with more freedom than ever before because any lack of vision is not my personal shortcoming but only a veil that will sooner or later be lifted by the miracle of the message of the Infinite Way and by the Grace of being placed in the life of my Guru who can truly say, "My will be done."*

*Thank you father...*

*Walter*

*P.S. In re-reading what I have just said it seems to sum up thus: I know I want to bring the Infinite Way to the Gentiles; yet I know I have no power of my own, but if MY power, YOUR power, functions within me there will be no end of activity and fulfillment—and that only when surrender is complete. If or until or now, I wait with growing peace and humility.*

When Joel answered the letter I felt an enormous release. He was in agreement with all I said and I felt that whatever the tension was between us, it had served its purpose. So when the class he was to give that summer in Hawaii approached, I was excited about playing my usual role of major domo, greeting people, running errands, and generally assisting in any way Joel wanted.

When the summer arrived, I went to Hawaii to attend Joel's class, the Hale Koa class. By this time Joel had married

Emma and they had purchased a big two-story home on the windward side of Oahu in a lush tropical area at the end of a road next to towering walls of volcanic rock. You entered from the upper floor. On the lower or basement floor there was a room that was large enough to accommodate the seventy or so people who had come to attend the class.

I remember Emma's showing me around the house when I arrived, and I was amused by the way she coyly pointed to the queen-size bed and said "this is where Joel and I sleep." I can't say that I was shocked, but I was surprised. Though I knew Joel was attracted to pretty feminine ladies, he had always seemed so asexual to me that this was the first time I had thought of him in that intimate context.

In preparation for the class I played my usual role. I would hang around the house answering telephone calls, arranging flowers, meeting people at the door, and going to the airport for special people. In the afternoon the day before the class began I was alone with Joel in his living room, and Joel once more asked me why I wouldn't teach in New York.

I wasn't completely honest with Joel about my true feelings. I knew that Floyd Nowell had taken over Joel's group in Maui at Joel's suggestion, and there had been a problem. When Joel visited the island he usurped Floyd's authority with the group and pulled the rug out from under him by making corrections and trying to improve on what Floyd was teaching. I didn't want that to happen to me. If I set myself up formally as an Infinite Way teacher, I might find myself in the same situation, so I avoided telling Joel my reason fearing his disapproval.

I tried to be more subtle and answered his question by telling him that my purpose in New York at present was just to keep the flame alive there for him, that I was like a candle flame, but when he came to town he was like a search light. To change the subject I added, "Joel, I have had two fathers, John in my theater and cultural world, and you in my spiritual world. Now John has been taken out of my life. I hope nothing happens to you."

Joel instantly became livid and springing off the couch where he was sitting, he turned to me with a look of anger on his face that I had never seen a hint of before, and said, "You want me to die! Get out of this house. Go back to New York. I don't want you in this class. Get out of this house." I was stunned. I had never seen him in a rage like this before. I tried to mumble apologies and attempted to clear the air but didn't know what to say, and he didn't give me a chance to explain, instead he literally pushed me to the front door. He slammed it after me with a bang. I stood on the front steps dumbfounded for quite a while, not knowing what to do. I was hoping he would open the door and I would find it was a bad dream. He didn't; so after a while I left.

At that time I was staying with Floyd Nowell, who lived close by. Floyd, whom I felt was my spiritual brother, was the only other male student into whom Joel had put so many years of time and energy. He saw Joel almost every day when Joel was in Hawaii and also, though respectful, was the only one who didn't seem a bit intimidated by Joel. After I told Floyd what had happened and how desperate I was feeling, he went over to Joel's office and interceded for me. He told Joel, "You can't do this to Walter. He's crushed. The Infinite Way is his whole life." After a while, Joel agreed to see me.

The next morning I went to Joel's office in his home. He sat across the desk from me without a trace of a smile and eyes that lacked compassion. I had never seen him with such a stern and unloving countenance before. I was abashed, and it made me feel that I had committed some unredeemable sin. If he had asked me to jump off a cliff I might have done it. In all the 12 years that I had known Joel up to this point he had never put me down or tried to discipline me before. I knew that people had come to him with speculations about my private life and such, but he shut them up and never even mentioned it to me. This time he said, "You don't understand a thing. Big lights, little lights, what's that got to do with it?" Then without knowing the details of what had previously taken place, he proceeded to attack me for being rude to one of the elderly students who had come to the class.

What had happened was this—when I was having appointments at the Infinite Way center in Los Angeles, anelderly woman had a couple of private appointments with me, and at the conclusion she told me that she was changing her will, leaving everything to me. I felt she was trying to buy my attention; so I counseled her that if she wanted to leave something to someone she shouldn't tell them about it; otherwise, it would put the relationship on a financial basis and could be interpreted as a bid for a personal relationship rather than a spiritual one.

When she arrived at the airport in Hawaii to attend the Hale Koa class, I met her and gave her a tour of the island. On the ride she suddenly said, "I did it." I said, "Did what?" She said, "I changed my will and left everything to you." Perhaps I shouldn't have, but her changing her will against my request really upset me, and I told her so. Apparently, after our ride she went to Joel and said I had been mean to her.

In my appointment with Joel he scolded me for upsetting the woman. I told him I was sorry if I falsely judged her, and that I should have handled it more spiritually. About this time tears came into my eyes. After I was thoroughly chastised, Joel said, "All right, you can stay for the class," and I was dismissed therewith. I was summarily relieved and, though still feeling that I had been put through an emotional wringer, I was determined to see what this unfortunate experience had to show me spiritually.

That night, before signaling for the tape recorder to be turned on, Joel told everyone to be sure to take advantage of the opportunity to meet and talk with the group leaders who were present. He pointed out Eileen Bowden from Victoria, Myrtle Howe from Seattle, Floyd Nowell from Hawaii, and on down the list skipping over New York, his largest group, as though I was not in the room. I sat in the back trying to pacify my emotions and hurt feelings by telling myself over and over, "Joel is God guided," and "there is but one power and one presence."

The day after the class I went to Joel's office to say goodbye, hoping he would send me off with a feeling that our break was temporary. Joel usually took me to the airport after a visit sending me home with his good wishes, but this time it was different. In a flat, cold, and chilling finality he said, "Goodbye," and that was it. I turned and walked out the door feeling more empty and alone than I ever had before. I was deserted by both of my fathers, John by death, Joel by rejection.

Except for the brief time when Joel gave a New York class the following year, our relationship remained strained. Inexplicably during that class, everything seemed to go back to the way had been in the past, before our relationship had changed. Joel was warm again, and he complimented me on how smoothly the class went and the first rate accommodations I had arranged. I recall one other warm and personal experience similar to those of the past that took place between Joel and me during that time.

After his final talk we were riding in a taxi on our way to a supper in a fashionable duplex apartment on Fifth Avenue owned by one of his students when a depleted and low-keyed Joel said, "I'm tired, so tired. Was the talk tonight all right?" I remember closing my eyes for a second, and I got the message about Joel that was so loud and clear that I had to say it out loud: "Well done, good and faithful servant. Thou hath been faithful in the few, now I will make you master of many." Joel seemed revitalized when we arrived at the apartment.

On my last meeting with Joel before he left town, suddenly the curtain came down again. It was as though a different person than the one he had been all week was now sitting in his chair. Once more there was a heavy solemnity about him and a stern frown on his face. I told him that I had decided to leave New York and retire to the little house I owned in Key West, and that I was going to let grace show me what was to come next. With a sense of frustration he lamented, "I hope you mean that." Then in an angry voice Joel said something that seemed to contradict his disapproval of me. He said, "Don't you realize that having you is like having someone who could be the president of General Motors." I didn't ask him what he meant by that but afterwards I thought about it and assumed he meant someone who could carry on a large operation and spread the word.

I knew it was time for me to leave New York because just before this final class, I had produced another play starring Tallulah Bankhead and Joan Blondell that led me to be consciously aware of what I valued most in life—my spiritual activities. The play, *Crazy October* by James Leo Herlihy, who wrote *Midnight Cowboy,* was not successful, and when I went into Sardi's I didn't really care what people thought or that it had failed. One's true religion is what that person cares most about, and, for me, finding God was that.

I was going to leave New York as soon as I took care of one more detail following the class. Willette Kershaw was a frail 90-year-old actress who had been successful until her retirement, and had been associated with the legendary actress, Sarah Bernhard. Willette left the theater many years before, she bought a house in Key West. When I was there I would visit her for tea on some afternoons and talk about her interest in the Infinite Way. Willette came to New York for that final class of Joel's, and during the class she had a heart attack. Everyone departed at the end of the class, and I was left to see that she was taken care of.

The doctors treated Willette in her hotel room because they said she was too frail to be moved to the hospital. One day the doctor heard her tell me that she wanted to go to Hawaii to be with Joel's people there. Startled, he motioned for me to meet him outside the room and said that the trip would kill her.

She kept insisting. I prayed over it and felt that she had nothing else to live for, and had no family other than the Infinite Way family; so if the trip was too much for her that would be as good a way for her to go as any. Therefore, I arranged her ticket, hired a limousine, went to the airport where I got permission to take her right to the plane, and off she flew. She arrived in Hawaii and lived on for what turned out to be a divinely inspired length of time.

Willette had told me that in her will she intended to leave everything in her estate to Joel; so when I returned to Key West I looked into her affairs and found that a highly suspect local lawyer who handled her affairs there had put everything she had, including her valuable waterfront house, into a phony corporation he owned. It was obvious that he had planned to take everything for himself when she died. When I asked for a prospectus of his corporation he stonewalled me, saying it was none of my business.

After I got my instructions through meditation, I decided to take a gamble. I phoned the lawyer and told him that I had friends in the U.S. Securities and Exchange Commission, and that I was going to have him investigated unless he signed everything back over to Willette. My bluff worked. He backed down and drew up the papers for her to sign. I sent them to Willette in Hawaii, asking her to get a lawyer in Honolulu to establish her compos mentis (i.e. sanity) sign the release, and return it immediately. She did what I asked, put the release in the mail—and died the next day!

When I heard that Willette had died, I thought my effort was all for nothing, but when her papers arrived back from Hawaii two days later, I immediately took them to the lawyer anyway. He hadn't yet heard the news; so he signed the release and gave me the deeds to register. I raced to the courthouse to file the papers, and afterwards went out on my boat.

When I returned home later that afternoon, my house had been ransacked and, as nothing was missing, I was certain it was the lawyer searching for the papers; fortunately, it was too late. Joel legally inherited Willette's estate, but when I told him what had transpired and how I had kept the crook from getting everything, Joel showed me no gratitude in return and told me I had no right to mess in his private affairs. Again I wondered why after 14 years of flawless communication, we were now so out of step with each other.

As time went on, I became more and more confused about how to correspond with Joel. He seemed to take everything I said or wrote the wrong way. For instance, I wrote Joel a letter in which I casually mentioned that "the social life in Key West is nil this year." I meant that I was spending more time meditating without the usual socializing. I thought

Joel would be pleased, but instead I got back a letter saying, "What social life? You are not supposed to have a social life."

That spring, as I began my 40th year, I received definite inner instructions telling me that I should go around the world and that when I arrived at the island of Ceylon, now Sri Lanka, I would have a life-changing experience. I thought it meant that I would be meditating in a Buddhist temple at this spot in the world that was the furthest from my Texas upbringing, and in the depths of my meditations the heavens would open up, a shaft of light would descend upon me, and I would experience nirvana. That didn't happen, but I did have a significant life-altering experience in Ceylon; just not in the way I expected.

It was in the summer of 1960 that I took off on my journey to Ceylon, planning to stay in Japan for a while on my way. When I arrived in Honolulu, Joel and Emma were in New York. Daisy Shigemura, the Japanese woman who led Joel's work in Hawaii, arranged a dinner party for me with a half dozen of her top students. In those days whenever I visited Infinite Way groups, I was treated like St. Paul visiting the Thessalonians.

Three times during the dinner Daisy said, "We are not worthy to walk the same earth as Joel Goldsmith." The third time she said it I couldn't keep my mouth shut and responded, "Daisy, that's not good Infinite Way. Joel says that we are heir and joint heir with Christ to all the heavenly riches." As soon as I said it, I wished I hadn't because the smile left Daisy's face and I knew she was upset at being corrected.

I don't know what Daisy said to Joel, but I found out later that she had called him in New York, and as a result I got a telegram from Joel that stung like a scorpion saying, "Do not identify yourself in Japan as representing me personally or the Infinite Way. Do not claim any association with the activity of the Infinite Way. I'm sure you will respect my wishes. Request otherwise pleasant journey on your personal pursuits."

Needless to say, I was crushed and totally bewildered. Joel had always said that as there was no organization no one could be excommunicated. I felt that was exactly what was happening to me. Anyway, how could I be excluded from an infinite way? Feeling empty, lonely, and frightened, I continued my journey.

On this trip I had decided not to make any advance contacts or seek names of people to contact, but rather to let consciousness or grace design the journey. On the way, I met someone on the beach in Hawaii who gave me the name of an American furniture manufacturer in Tokyo. I called him upon my arrival. He suggested he stop by my hotel for a cocktail after work. I passed muster and he invited me out to his house in Shibuya, a fashionable part of Tokyo, for dinner. Later he told me that his wife was on an around-the-world trip for a few months and suggested that if I would rent his house for that time, he would like to stay in a hotel for a change. Grace really out-performed itself. With a charming house, a houseboy, and a cook, I lived in great style, became a good friend of the top Japanese author of the day, Yukio Mishima, and was immediately introduced to a number of the leading people in the arts and theater in Tokyo.

One incident of a significantly spiritual nature took place that had an enormous impact on me and contributed to the life-changing experience I had in Ceylon later on. Though I usually went to Chinjuku-ku, the Greenwich Village of Tokyo, for my nightlife, one evening I decided to go down to the Ginza, the Times Square of Tokyo, to see a movie. Standing in line at a little yakitori restaurant in an alley off the Ginza, where they serve seasoned rice with chicken, roasted ginkgo nuts, and other delicious things on little skewers, I began talking to a young Japanese man who was fluent in English. During our conversation he asked if I had been to Kamakura where the famous, often-photographed giant iron Buddha sits. I said I hadn't and, as the following day was my new friend's day off, he suggested that if I wanted to go he would be my guide.

The next morning we met and got on the train. After an hour or so the train slowed down, and my friend said, "We get off here." We did, and to my surprise we weren't in a train station but on a dirt path with a sign saying "Kita Kamakura," which meant north Kamakura. The train moved on, and not more than three feet from the other side of the tracks was an ancient gate leading up to a complex of Zen temples dating back to the 8th Century. As we walked up the hill on a centuries-worn stone path to the main temple, everything in me began to stir. Just inside the entrance of this majestic building with its pagoda roofs and time-dulled gold trimmings was a small room with a tea table. My friend left me there and disappeared, only to return with the master of the temple.

The master had a time-defying face, wrinkled but ageless, enhanced by a gray goatee and piercing eyes. His smile was gentle and welcoming as he motioned me to join him in a cup of tea. For a few minutes we sat in silence. Finally, in a low guttural broken English that seemed to come from deep inside of him, the master asked, "You want meditate?" I, of course, said, "By all means," and he led my friend and me into the main sanctuary where we knelt on our knees before the altar Japanese style. We meditated for some 45 minutes, and for me the meditation was so intense that I felt the top of my head was about to come off. The Spirit coursed through my body toe-to-head in a way it hadn't since my arrival in Japan.

When we finished meditating we returned to the tea room and the master reappeared. As we partook of another cup of tea, he turned to me and in a deep commanding voice said, "This you home. You stay." I began to shake my head and he kept repeating, "This you home. You stay."

Everything inside of me turned to jelly. I tried to explain the reason I could not stay, but the words would not come out, and all I could say was that I could not. Though I ached to stay, I knew deep inside of me I had lived in a monastery, perhaps this one, in a past life and that this time around I had to find my answers in today's world, not escape from it. The master repeated, "Any time, you come, this you home." I regretfully said my goodbyes and managed to get outside before I broke into a flood of tears.

I began to cry from my eyes, my nose, and what seemed like my ears as well. I felt as though the love of my life was in a house somewhere in the city and I did not know where to look, or that my home was on some street and I could not find it.

Still hurting from the sting of Joel's rejection, what I felt from this experience was similar to what I had felt after reading Joel's letter in Amsterdam, and it re-established my realization that I was called to the mystical approach, that my whole being had to be filled with God. This time I experienced it in a different context than the Infinite Way.

# My Breakthrough

After several more months in Japan, I continued on to Ceylon, making stops in Hong Kong and Thailand. I finally arrived and checked into an old English hotel on the outskirts of Colombo. Instead of feeling that I was nearing my spiritual destiny, I staggered into my room feeling sick to my stomach and suffering from a high fever. I did what I usually do in such circumstances; I tried to meditate, make my contact, and see if I could heal myself. Ordinarily, when that does not work, I call someone I consider to be high in consciousness for their grace, but there wasn't anyone I could call; so I decided to render unto Caesar the things which are Caesar's and asked the hotel to send me a physician. One came and gave me sulfa drugs, which was all they had in those pre-penicillin pre-antibiotic days.

For the next six days I lay in my hotel bed with my life flashing before me. I was literally at the end of the road. The doctor would check in on me daily, but otherwise the only people I saw were the dark silent hotel employees who brought me soup or changed the bed linens. During this time my fever would fluctuate from 101 degrees to 103 degrees. As the days progressed, I felt weaker and weaker. After a few days of this high fever, the doctors began to think that perhaps I had contracted typhoid fever. As it turned out, I had to be strapped down by this extreme condition in order for me to do what I had to do; otherwise I would most likely have put it off.

Day by day, as my whole life passed before me everything boiled down to one thing: my relationship with Joel. Sick as I was, I got out the small Swiss portable typewriter that I had bought in Hong Kong and propped myself up in bed with it on my lap. After an intense meditation I decided to put my feelings on paper in the form of a letter to Joel, even though I thought I probably wouldn't mail it. I knew that no matter how carefully I explained what I felt, if Joel read the letter it would cause a big explosion, but I had to write it.

The minute I finished the letter the fever that had remained for almost a week was totally gone! That seemed to be a divine message telling me to actually mail the letter; so being afraid that I would get cold feet and not do it if I waited until the next day, I walked down the hall in my bathrobe and posted it. I kept a copy of that important letter because I knew it marked a turning point in my spiritual journey. As I read it now, it still affects me. I am amazed at the ferocity with which I lashed out at my pain.


*November 27, 1960*

*Dear Joel,*


*After three full months in Japan, I came here directed by the feeling that this would be a good week to set aside for rest and recollections. I did not realize how prophetic the idea was—I have not left my room for six days as I arrived with a fever of some strange kind.*

*I have done lots of examination and listening these days, and uppermost in my mind has been my relationship with you and the recent non- or ex-communication. There is no need to recall my history with you as it now covers 15 years back to the first visit when John was writing the introduction to the Infinite Way, the meditation that opened me up in Detroit, the revelations on Maui, the letter from you written on what you called your "holiest night of my life" in which you said it had been shown you that I was called to mysticism and so much more.*

*Except for brief moments, the past three years had been strange and different. You have been led to project an attitude toward me of considerable dissatisfaction with me, personal failure, incompetence, and almost loathing. For almost three years you haven't meditated with me personally as you used to do and little I could do would please you. I have tried to refuse to see our conflict in human terms, because I have felt that obviously you were led to do what you have done, and I never doubt your guidance though I can't understand it. I have tried not to defend myself, resist evil, or seek personal justification. As you know, I have been much alone the past three years; so just a bit of affection, a pat on the head for effort, or some encouragement would have been appreciated, but so strongly have I felt God's hand behind it that I have kept relatively (for me) quiet. I have also felt that words meant little and results more, and I was willing to stand on my history of results in the I.W. leading right up to this past spring....After the class the group in Washington asked me to come for a visit—I answered the call and was more than gratified with the experience and the attitude such people as Economos and others had toward my presentation. They asked me to return but my "listening" felt not for now; so I declined, but that wasn't trusted because when you were approached on the idea of my coming whatever you said resulted in their writing me withdrawing the invitation. Also I felt that there was something I had to do in Key West and found it was the job over Willette's estate which was saved only by listening to no one but guidance... Yet even these things have had somewhat of a tang of wrongness to you.*

*I don't think I have ever disgraced the Infinite Way or your name in the past, nor represented it unwisely. I certainly have never represented myself as your official spokesman, nor went anywhere without your permission... and never never tried to use the name of the Infinite Way for personal gains of ego or otherwise...So when I received your cable in Hawaii I could not help but feel it was a highly unnecessary remonstration and worded in a cutting manner to one who has shown no history of deceit... "DO NOT IDENTIFY YOURSELF IN JAPAN AS REPRESENTATIVE ME PERSONALLY OR THE INFINITE WAY. DO NOT CLAIM ANY ASSOCIATION WITH THE ACTIVITY OF THE INFINITE WAY. I'M SURE YOU WILL RESPECT MY WISHES (as though there would be any doubt) REQUEST OTHERWISE PLEASANT JOURNEY ON YOUR PERSONAL PURSUITS." Knowing how cold the first part of the cable is, the last part sounds rather hypocritical.*

*Indeed, you had written me I could not go to Japan with you, but also you knew that way back in England we had discussed Japan and I said I had the vision to go at the end of the summer, and "it" felt to go, but I expected the respect of those who know me not to attribute ulterior motives to my actions, and I did not feel you meant for me not to go at all. Frankly I had hoped I could at least see you while there, that was all.*

*Now, the same Spirit that has led to the writings of the Infinite Way and its healings has guided the cable you sent as well; so what is the meaning of it? Do you feel there is something to be afraid of? Is there a power that can operate against the Infinite Way? Is there an organization that needs protection? Perhaps it is shaping up that way.*

*I know as well as anything that ultimately there will be a world with no separation between students and teachers, and all mankind will have daily activity as well as those within the few who are drawn together daily to share the light of consciousness, but in the meantime there is a need of schooling—with schools there is always the danger of staying in school too long, becoming a grotesque, and falling under law. Last year the message not only reached a height but the consciousness was indeed projected into the students; however, simultaneously there are those who are subtly steering toward organization…Perhaps it is supposed to be that the seeds of such are to be sewn into I.W. as they were into C.S. for the same reasons as there… that I don't know.*

*Perhaps those around you could become*

*as intimidated or frightened of you as those who were around M.B.E....I do know that few apart from Emma, Bess, and Floyd really tell you their full feelings.*

*That is why I was surprised at the lack of understanding last summer. When I heard Daisy say over and over to the students that they were not "worthy to walk the same earth as Joel Goldsmith," I couldn't help but remind her that we learn equally that "I of my own self can do nothing" and "I can do all things through Christ" (though I personally lean most strongly on the first). And after five times of her saying "If you were oriental you would understand" to her students, or "occidentals don't understand"—my mind flashed back to the lesson of three years ago when you hit me hard for a similar statement...I said to you at that time that when you come to N.Y. it was like a searchlight, and I was a candle next to you. You said, "Big lights, little lights... superstition...You don't begin to understand the Infinite Way." And you were so right. There is a world of difference between mouthing words and realizing the fabric of oneness...That is why it does no good to say "Now you are teachers." Only demonstration can show that.*

*Of course, to the world I appear as Shylock or Hamlet, and only the spiritually enlightened realize that what they see is only the makeup and costume and I am no more to be judged by appearances than any other. But I'm not a child anymore, and for some reason that I can only attribute to the things I believe in and live by, people have grown in the past few years to treat me with considerable respect, doors open, and I am accepted everywhere my feet take me. I am ready to spend my life giving whatever I have to give wherever it is wanted. But such as I am, this is it, and if you distrust it, feel compelled to judge it by appearances, and feel me unable to help without changes that must be beyond my power, than you had better reject me.*

*If you no longer want me as one of your household I will accept that, but within I know you are my God-given Guru and that whatever heaven has joined no man can put asunder. But I shall never leave you of choice, and never have. If the I.W. is to slip into organization, and many groups are now preaching law already, then my Spirit would conflict. But no matter under what title the truths are called, there will be those whose lives are dedicated to them and rest assured I am one. I shall not betray those truths because they are you.*

*I am trying to be simple and open, Joel. I want to do whatever you want, I want to serve the truths you have revealed, but I don't want you to be unhappy with me or disappointed with me nor expecting me to change in some future time that isn't now. I have great love and affection for you humanly and spiritually, and will be joyously a member of your house if you wish, but if it must be a relationship of scorn and mistrust, then it isn't a relationship at all.*

*I could never represent you nor teach the message living under fear that constantly I might displease you or bring condemnation down on myself. Practicing what I have been taught, I daily release everything and everybody—God, you, the Infinite Way, and myself.*

*Always and with all Love,*

*Walter*

After posting the letter, that night I had the most important, prophetic dream of my life. Basically, I believe that Carl Jung was accurate in saying that the people you dream about signify those characteristics in yourself that they symbolize; however, I also believe that dreams can sometimes contain significant spiritual messages, and this one did.

Shaken from my lengthy illness and needing to find some place to get my strength back before I could even begin to explore my dream, I changed my plane ticket scheduled for a stop in India and went straight to the Greek Island of Poros, where I checked into a quiet, family-run hostel.

After a few days of recuperation, one morning my inner voice told me to take my diary and go to the top of the mountain behind the house. As I sat there at peace looking out over the miraculously blue Aegean water, the dream began to take shape.

I had dreamed that I was in a grand Gothic cathedral. I was dressed in an oriental monk's robe with a Bible in one hand and a begging bowl in the other. I felt humble and awe-struck as I walked down to the altar rail hoping with all my heart that I would be accepted in the order and be allowed to take my vows to become a monk.

On the other side of the altar were a half-dozen black robed, gray faced, inquisitional priests. When I pleaded with them to let me join the order they sneered at me and told me to leave. I cried and begged them to accept me. The half dozen funereally robed priests went into something like a football huddle, and when they came out of it the cadaverous leader then turned to me and said, "All right, we will give you one chance. We will accept you if you go out into the world, meditate on, contemplate, and discover the sin of Jesus"— the sin of Jesus!

I can now look back and see with clarity that the dream symbolized my "double thread" concept that began at the crater in Hawaii and has been the theme of my life ever since. Sitting there on the Greek island in the Fall of 1960 I wrote:

> *Today, I am joyous over what the dream has revealed. Though I have claimed that God is the only power, I, like Jesus, have denied it by desiring to help others. Only self doubt could make me feel the need to be useful, to show others, and to prove that God is. Joint heirdom is possible, is now, because Jesus had the same sin as I, was indeed as me.*
>
> *To sin means to fall short of the mark, of perfection. Jesus' sin was personal responsibility. Though he knew there was nothing to hinder anyone, "Take up your bed and walk," and though he knew that there was no power other than God, he still felt that he had to save the world—from what? He believed the world needed saving and that he could save it, as Joel did, and as I do.*
>
> *This is the most subtle sin, yet at the same time it is the negative that makes the light*

shine for man to "see" by. Perhaps man would not be infinite without including sin; perhaps this sin is Jesus' bridge, his cross, his virtue, and his destruction as well. In anticipating his crucifixion Jesus violated his teaching by "taking thought for the morrow." Every man may do this, but the longer he can stay thinking in terms of "now," not in terms of personal responsibility, which can only be in the future, he is closer to pure truth and his God self.

You can never betray a person unless that person possesses a sin to be betrayed by. Jesus could never have been and was never betrayed by Judas; rather he made his crucifixion possible by his own belief in personal responsibility, by believing he had to personally fulfill the Scriptures at some future time. He betrayed himself. But his betrayal of himself was the greatest gift possible, because it made it possible for all mankind to be equal to him and free.

The only safeguard against self and world betrayal is in ratio as one stays pure in NOW and therefore free of self doubt which only rises by being out of "now." One who has found God lives in mystical aloneness, complete as long as they can stay in now without help from without.

The only way to avoid the sin of Jesus is by emptying. To pray without ceasing is to be constantly empty. Empty, empty, empty. The power of the confessional is that it empties. When we are empty we are completely in the now and there is nothing to create any power for all is.

*The sin of Jesus is also what has been falsely done in his name. His message has at times been distorted by organized religions, compromised by manmade restrictions, misinterpreted by leaders who seek control, and has been used to subjugate individual rights.*

My dream told me that I had bought into superstition and tradition myself by wanting to belong to the order the priests in the dream represented. I realized that though Joel had no formal organization, my desiring to belong to the Infinite Way was the same as wanting to join a church. My passion for feeling the presence of God had to be fulfilled from within my own inner cathedral of spirit and not from any formulized outside teaching or system.

A couple of months after I returned home to Key West, where I had settled after New York, I gradually became aware of an amazing outcome that resulted from my experience in Ceylon. When I was in my junior and senior years in college I worked on the radio. I would get up early to bring the station on the air, attend my classes at the university, study in the afternoons, stay up late at night, and burn the proverbial candle at both ends. As a result I began to have migraine headaches similar to those that Joel and Mary Baker Eddy experienced at one point in their lives. Every month or two I would be racked with a painful migraine, and nothing I tried would faze them.

After I began my spiritual search, sometimes I could catch the migraines early on and through meditation keep them from happening. But most often I could not. I would walk around holding my head feeling as though it was in a tightening vice until the pain became so intense that I would eventually start to vomit and vomit. Finally, I would fall asleep, sleep for at least ten hours, and wake feeling fine—until the next one. If I drank more than a little wine or partook of a couple of alcoholic drinks, it would often bring a migraine on. Several months after I returned home from Ceylon, I suddenly realized something amazing. I had not had another one since before I wrote the letter to Joel. And in fact, to this day I have not had another.

I believe that the reason the migraines stopped was that before I wrote that letter to Joel, I was not able to let my pent-up energy flow out from within me. Before then I turned that bottled-up energy in on myself, and not having an outlet for it resulted in my headaches. Spiritually, until I was willing to live by that which I had within myself, I wasn't truly loving myself, and my migraines were the price I paid. It was also interesting that after Joel left Christian Science and went out on his own, he too no longer had migraines.

After Joel received the letter I wrote him from Ceylon, he did something uncharacteristic that surprised me because it went against his principle of not giving unasked-for advice. Out of the blue, Joel wrote my mother telling her that I was in a disturbing state of mind and that she should be concerned. I had written mother from Japan about my exciting time there and my plans for the future on my return. She couldn't have been happier with or about me and wondered what Joel was talking about.

After Joel received my letter from Ceylon, when people would ask him, "How's Walter?" he would say, "He's not with us any more." My being considered *persona non grata* spread. Nevertheless, from that point on I continued to receive Joel's monthly letter, corresponded with Floyd and Lorene McClintock who kept me in touch with Joel's activities, and he would hear about my mine from various people; so we were never completely out of contact, but for the next two years I was not a part Joel's work.

One of my dilemmas during this period was deciding what to contribute to financially. For years I had sent checks, or what might be called my tithes, to Joel regularly. When I was an actor I sent him $200 or $300 checks, when I became a successful producer I often sent him a $1,000 or more at a time. Joel used to shake his head and say that he had millionaires who didn't give as much. Now, because he was so dissatisfied with me, I didn't feel right about sending him any money personally. I didn't want him to think I was trying to bribe my way back into his good graces. So I meditated, and what came to me was this. Though I was having trouble with Joel, I still believed heart and soul in the Infinite Way message; so instead of sending money to Joel I sent it to his book department, which supplied prisons and libraries with *Infinite Way* books.

A few months after my Ceylon experience, Joel began a series of classes that took him across the United States, then to England, and ultimately to South Africa. His wife, Emma, and Daisy, the Japanese woman who conducted the work in Hawaii, accompanied him to give him support. After England they went to Rome, intending to get visas for South Africa. Because Daisy was of Japanese descent and apartheid was still in force refusing entry for people of any color, she was denied a visa.

Joel was furious, but because there was nothing he could do he sent the women back to Hawaii, and he went to South Africa alone.

As I said earlier, at his classes Joel always had a number of the inner family with him for support. Though none of us were consciously aware of what our prayers and energies contributed to the work, its absence may have affected what took place when he had to present a mystical message in the apartheid climate that prevailed in darkest South Africa at that time. Half way through the class Joel had a heart attack and ended up in the hospital.

I heard about Joel's illness via a letter I received from Gertrude de Kock shortly after it took place. Gertrude was a remarkable no-nonsense metaphysical teacher who lived in Johannesburg and had a large following there. On a trip to New York she had dined with Joel and me, attended a couple of his lectures, later miraculously spent time in the small Texas town that my family came from, and our friendship grew. Gertrude wrote that she had gone to see Joel in the hospital and that he had refused to accept the fact that he had had a heart attack. Instead, he made every kind of excuse for being there.

Gertrude's letter made me sad and reminded me of how much I loved Joel, the man. I knew what a shock the experience must have been for him and how he would deny it, not so much for himself as in defense of his healing message.

When Joel was able to travel, he returned to Hawaii and proceeded to hide the human truth from as many of his students as possible, just as most of the old time metaphysicians did in those days. They were afraid that if their followers saw them being human they would not believe their messages; so Joel sent out a letter saying that his guidance had told him to cancel all of his scheduled lectures for the rest of the year. He didn't say, "I've had a heart attack," because he knew quite well that people did not expect, nor did they want, their leaders to have the problems they said could be avoided; otherwise, their teachings would seem invalid.

Three times during his career Joel had lost a number of his followers because his humanity showed, and he didn't want that to happen again. When he left Christian Science many of his old following disowned him; when he divorced Nadea another group broke off, and when he married Emma still others were faced with his humanity and left his following. That is why Joel didn't announce that he had had a heart attack.

Walter's favorite picture of Joel.

Walter with leis from Hawaii.

CHAPTER NINE

# Rapprochement

*W*hen I returned to Key West from Ceylon after going around the world, I felt more lost than ever. My 40th birthday arrived, and I had always believed that when I reached forty I would begin some kind of public spiritual work, perhaps something similar to Joel's. As it was, I didn't see any possibility on my horizon. Joel had cut me off from the Infinite Way family, and there wasn't any formal organization I wanted to be connected with. Although my theater friends liked hearing me talk about metaphysical or spiritual matters, and some would even ask me for counseling, nothing was shaping up that could resemble a profession.

After several very unhappy months I began to wonder if my belief that at forty I would enter a new and more spiritual phase of my life was no more than wishful thinking. I still hadn't found any clue as to why my break with Joel had happened. Finally, on the day of my 40th birthday I received my answer.

I was reading Dr. Carl Jung's autobiographical book, *Memories, Dreams, Reflections,* and read of an encounter that he and his teacher, Freud, had on a trip they made to America together. It was an archetypal explanation for what had transpired between Joel and me, and it explained a necessary stage in the maturation of most mentor/student or father/son relationships. One morning Jung told Freud about a dream he had had the night before. Freud got angry, blew up, and said, "You want me to die," the same words Joel had said to me. From that day on their relationship was not the same, just as Joel's and mine was never quite the same again.

In the animal world there inevitably comes a time when the young lion has to challenge the pride's leader and either take over, or go out and start his own family. It's basically the same in the human world. Both Freud and Joel may not have been consciously aware of what caused them to instinctively react as they did to Jung and me, but in both cases they were performing the greatest act of love possible by forcing their consciousness-sons to make the break and discover their own individuality. The time had come for their sons to be independent so that they could ultimately become interdependent. Though the son's messages were built on the foundation their spiritual fathers had laid for them, they had to define their own unique interpretations in order to make them their own.

Jung also made the statement that "life begins at 40," that at 40 we break with our fathers and start living out of our own consciousness. It makes no difference if our birth-fathers died when we were two or if they are still alive. At 40 years of age the time has come to end our reliance on our gurus, teachers, or father figures to tell us how to live, and we must start living from our own consciousness. Both Jung and I were 40 when that happened.

When I realized that what happened to Jung and me was a natural process, something wonderful took place. I was able to impersonalize my break with Joel and be free of any sense of blame on either of our parts. However, more important was the realization that it was a mistake to look at Joel as though he was a man. Joel was not a man; he was a state of consciousness. He was the most God-guided person I have ever known.

Joel did whatever his inner guidance told him to do without always knowing the human reasons for what he did. He never contemplated nor was he aware of the price he might have to pay personally for following his guidance. He didn't figure things out psychologically in order to accomplish a desired result. He simply did what his inner intuitive guidance directed. As confusing and inconsistent with his teachings as some of his actions seemed at times, without exception they resulted in divine outcomes.

I realized that by treating me the way he had in those painfully confusing years, Joel had given me the greatest gift a person can possibly receive. He kicked me out of the nest so that I would stand on my own spiritual feet. Most of Joel's inner circle never received that freedom, but instead spent the rest of their lives saying, "Joel said, Joel said." I was blessed by his sometimes tough love.

I now know, and I have been told by others who were close to Joel, that it took a lot out of him to be so rough on me. It was as painful for him, if not more so, than it had been for me. I was the son Joel always wanted. I was a clean-cut college graduate, a Christian boy from an upper middle class family, heir to all the advantages of my upbringing. Joel had a dream that, like a son stepping into and following his father's profession, I would carry on his passion and continue his

Infinite Way work. Perhaps, somewhat like a son, I have tried, but I have only been able to do it in my own way, in my own time, and in my own words.

# The Miracle

Now that I felt that I was to live purely out of my own consciousness, I knew I had to first prove myself and my principles in the marketplace before any spiritual work would come about. During the next two years everything I touched seemed to turn to gold. I pictured how the old waterfront in Key West could be fixed up as a tourist attraction where the cruise ships could dock, and I had an artist friend paint sketches of my concept. I got the city to fund the project, and it became the now famous Mallory Square. I wrote the by-laws and helped found the Old Island Restoration Foundation, which became responsible for the preservation of the old part of the island and the success that followed. To boost the restoration project I bought an old rundown building across from the waterfront and restored it.

A friend of mine who designed and produced silk-screened fabrics suggested that the building would be an ideal place to put in a fabric printing operation, with space for ninety-foot printing tables on the second floor and a showroom at ground level. I knew that such an artistically stimulating operation would quickly become a tourist attraction.

There was also a spiritual purpose for offering the public the experience of watching art being produced by hand. I remembered Emerson's famous essay, *Self-Reliance*, warning us about losing our self respect by becoming too dependent on machines to do everything for us. Seeing brightly colored, beautiful fabrics being printed by hand down the long tables, rather than by machines ,would make those who watched the process proud of being human.

Shortly thereafter I was in Palm Beach and met Lily Pulitzer, who came from an extremely rich family, married into the Pulitzer clan, and was a leader in the young Palm Beach set. For her own comfort Lily had created a lined shift dress that was cut to the knees giving her the freedom she wanted. Friends wanted copies; so she hired a couple of seamstresses to make them up. I saw the potential in what she was doing and talked her into coming down to Key West to see the factory. She hopped on her private plane, arrived, bought 26 rolls of fabric, then went to Miami, leased a dress-making factory, and was in business. Lily's friends were the heads of Harper's Bazaar and Vogue. They did photo shoots, publicized her line of clothing, and in no time there were Lily Pulitzer shops in the top resorts across the country and my silkscreen factory was an enormous success. The Lily Pulitzer line still exists forty-five years later.

As a result of the business that my factory brought to Key West, and because I had been instrumental in starting the Old Island Restoration Foundation, I was made Citizen of the Year in Key West, and feature articles were printed in the local papers. One editorial even had the headline "Starcke Deserves Honor." I cut all the clippings out and sent them to Joel, partly out of devilishness and partly hoping it would heal our break. His response was a spirit-lifting surprise, and it gave me hope that we could once more communicate.

After receiving the clippings, on March 19, 1963 Joel wrote me a letter that made my heart sing, He said, "Indeed, you have already fulfilled the years of your study and justified the teaching given to you." He said that not everyone was going to respond in the same fashion, that not everyone was going to leave the professional or business world in order to teach nor that it was necessary. In fact, he said that he saw a future time when there would be no such thing as separate ministries, but that people would live their spiritual lives in the arts and industry.

Joel said, "The important thing is that you made a success of your life," not only in the business world but also in my civic activities. He said that in this was full and complete success, and was a "showing forth of your spiritual capacities in a tangible form." He ended the letter saying that "It is a joy always to hear from you and to write to you." I knew from his letter that whatever it was that we had gone through had served its purpose.

Later that year I resigned from the presidency of the silkscreen factory and decided to go around the world again because I had another business idea I wanted to check out in Japan. At least, I thought that was the major reason. I hadn't seen Joel since his heart attack and wanted to re-establish some new kind of relationship on the way. I also looked forward to spending a few days with Floyd Nowell, but the powers that be sent me to Hawaii in order to experience something far more important, if not miraculous.

When I arrived in Hawaii I called up Joel to see if and when I could visit him. Since his heart attack he was seeing almost no one apart from Emma, Daisy, and Bess Anderson. He agreed to see me, and I went over to his side of the island to meet him in his home office.

As I sat across the desk from Joel, I could see that he was obviously an ill man. His skin was gray, his eyes expressionless. He was wearing sandals, and I saw that his feet were purple with bad circulation. Oddly, I felt completely removed from any feeling. Joel was very low key, rather listless, and he treated me as though I was someone who had read one of his books and had managed to arrange an appointment with him. It was strange experience. We talked impersonally for a while without mentioning our relationship or the past until finally he said, "Come back tomorrow," and got up to show me to the door.

The next day our time alone together again was a replay of the first meeting, low key, impersonal, and flat. Once more, he said to return the following day. On the evening before the third visit I was alone in an apartment in a high rise out on Diamond Head where I was staying with a friend who was away for the evening. Before going to bed I went out onto the balcony overlooking the ocean and lights in the distance to meditate. I remember that meditation as if it happened yesterday. I felt as though I were falling through space. It wasn't a blackness but a void, a total no-thing-ness. Afterwards, I knew that what had happened to me was extremely significant.

When I arrived at Joel's office the morning after my profound meditation I couldn't wait to tell him about my experience. I can't say that what took place that night had anything to do with my presence, but I was blessed to be there, and I felt, "Rejoice that your name is writ in heaven" for witnessing what had happened.

As I began to talk, the whole feeling in the room was different than it had been previously. Joel seemed glad to see me; he had a twinkle in his eye and a smile on his face. It was like old times. When I began to tell him about my medi-tation he interrupted me with warmth and affection and said, "Walter, I died last night, and it came to Emma that this is my ascension."

Within the hour the phone began to ring non-stop. Several of Joel's top students called out of the blue asking "What's going on out there? I feel I must come immediately," and they did. By the next day about eight people arrived.

We all crowded around the desk in Joel's little office, and he began to teach with the energy and spirit he had had years before. He was literally born again right before our eyes. The color returned to his face, his eyes brimmed with excitement, and Joel was back. Only his inner circle knew about his heart attack, and he hadn't told his general following; so, unfortunately, he couldn't now share his re-birth.

The lectures that followed Joel's comeback constituted the 1963 Kailua tapes. The second tape was titled *Above the Law to Grace,* which is listed on page 58 of Joel's tape catalogue.

Though the tape remains one of Joel's most powerful tapes, one had to be present when the message came through Joel to experience the full impact of the consciousness that was generated and transmitted to those who were there in his presence. In the tape he didn't just repeat what it means to live by grace. Joel led us into the very consciousness of what it means to move from a life lived by laws to one lived by experiencing grace as a way of life.

I was sitting no more than six feet from Joel across the desk and felt so drawn into the world of Spirit that I couldn't keep my eyes open as he spoke, but every time I did open them it was as though Joel was speaking directly to me. After that, the past slipped away, and we were no longer student and teacher. There was just oneness, and my tongue was untied. I was able to share my thoughts and feelings on a far more equal basis than ever before without the fear of his disapproval.

On that trip Joel said something I entered in my dairy that, looking back on it in retrospect, showed he was contemplating his departure from this plane and hinted at the short time he had left on earth. He said in substance, "Ten years after I die in some respects the Infinite Way will no longer be the Infinite Way, because just by the nature of things, it will be frozen off where I left it and the words I left it in. In order to stay alive it will have to be expressed in new ways and new words."

# Joel's Final Years

𝒜 week after Joel's rebirth I left Hawaii and continued on my way around the world. After what had happened in Hawaii, I knew that I didn't want to put my energy into another business project but rather return to Joel's work and spiritual pursuits. All I could think of was the freedom I felt and a sense of Joel's love.

After his rebirth, Joel immediately started giving classes again and as spirit would have it, he and Emma arrived in London for a class at the same time I arrived there from the Orient. I assisted him once more and it was like old times.

Shortly after, I returned to the States and had a close brush with history. It was 1963. The country was full of hope and new energy reflected by the handsome young president in the White House. I came to Texas to visit my mother in San Antonio and went up to see my sister in Austin and to attend the banquet for President Kennedy that was to take place that night after his stop in Dallas. My sister was to sit next to Kennedy, because her husband, a Methodist minister, was to give the eulogy. In anticipation, that afternoon we turned on the television and witnessed the assassination.

In response to my letter about the assassination, I received a letter from Joel on December 13 saying that "I told you in London that something of an enormous nature had taken place within you, and I am sure you felt that both

Emma and I recognized it." He then went on commenting about the assassination and how shocked he was that it could happen to any American president. He said that he had his students doing specific work of a protective nature because he had told them right after the election "that it was not likely that he (Kennedy) would live out his first term, and just two months ago I again told Emma that his time was drawing short." He added that he was sure I knew that the source of these intuitions was not God, but rather a vision that went beyond the normal reasoning capacity.

A few months passed, during which time I received some more awards that I forwarded to Joel, and I received another letter on March 17, 1964 from Joel saying that my success in Key West did not surprise him because I had shown that I was being led by something greater than my human selfhood, and therefore nothing was impossible.

Joel then added that I should remember that back in the Hollywood days he had told me that my days as an actor were over and I soon entered the producing world. In typical fashion he said that when the spiritual inspiration touched me it had no intention of letting me rest on my laurels; so he felt that it was actually the Spirit that touched me and moved me from New York City to a worldwide activity. He followed that with a personal touch that really moved me. He said "While I personally had nothing to do with this, I do feel that your contact with the Infinite Way made all of this inevitable." He ended the letter with his and Emma's love and the assurance that he was always close at hand.

I wrote him back a letter commenting on his statement about my progress and his saying that he had nothing to do with it. During our difficult period he would have jumped on me for writing what I did. I said:

*To answer your letter, I have to ask who is Joel Goldsmith, what is the Infinite Way, and who is Walter Starcke? Joel Goldsmith is a state of consciousness out of which a teaching and a collection of truths called the Infinite Way has come. There is no way you can separate the two any more than you can separate Jesus from the Christ. Walter Starcke is someone who has been transformed by the truths of the Infinite Way and to the degree that he lives those truths he is the Infinite Way.*

I got a letter back from Joel dated April 13, 1964 that instead of hopping on me for my presumptuous letter said, "It is a joyous experience to witness your continuous unfoldment," and then he outlined the extensive worldwide jaunt he was to begin on May 12. He was to start in Seattle, then to Chicago, and after that to England, Holland, Sweden, three cities in Germany, and two cities in Switzerland ending August 9. He pointed out that he was presently working on an entirely different turn. The message had started twelve years before, but stopped the day it started. Now (since his dark period in London where he said he had another notch to go) it was reactivated and was contained in *Living Between Two Worlds*. He said that he was reluctant to travel, but that his trip promised to be the most unusual trip he ever made during his Infinite Way life. Then for the first time he specifically asked me to do something, he asked me to come to the Chicago class, because if I would I would be at home with the old "gang."

To me, it was indeed the most unusual trip he had ever made, because I feel that *Living Between Two Worlds* opened the way for my Double Thread message. It made me feel that by Joel's often sending me post cards of the crater on Maui he was acknowledging the fact that reconciling the two commandments of cause and effect was, for me, the answer.

# The Last Days

After Joel's letter asking me to come to Chicago, I was torn. I wanted to go but I had a business negotiation in Key West to purchase a piece of property and didn't feel right about walking out on it at contract-signing time. I was grounded in the belief that everything that happens, happens in divine order; therefore, I believed that if I was supposed to be present at the class, matters would take care of themselves. They did! Without notice, the other party to the business deal cancelled by leaving the island without notice the day before the class was to begin; so I got the next plane to Chicago and went to the Statler Hotel where the lectures were to take place. When I checked in, I called Joel and he surprised me by exclaiming, "You didn't tell me you were coming!" I hadn't written to him whether I would be there or not, but the way he commented on my arrival showed me he really wanted me there. He told me to come to his suite right away.

This class was different than his other classes from the beginning to the end, and the way he set it up showed that consciously or unconsciously he was preparing for his departure. This was the first time he shared the platform with other speakers. He had chosen the five women teachers of the Infinite Way to make presentations, with his speaking at the beginning and ending of the class. Also, at his other appearances he would have ten or fifteen minute appointments with as many as he could crowd in between sessions. This time everyone felt that this was a special time and no one even asked for an appointment.

Before going down to the platform on the opening night, the five women speakers, Emma, and I all met in Joel's suite. The students from Hawaii arrived with a box of orchid leis and began putting them around Joel's, Emma's, and the five teachers' necks. When they came to me they slipped one over my head and a shock went through me. It was like a hot coal. I immediately took it off and, thanking them, said, "No, no." Though I had been absent from the work for over two years, there were enough people there who knew who I was so that if I, the only other man, had worn the lei like the others my name would have been passed around, and I didn't want to imply I was seeking to emulate Joel or claim to be heir apparent.

After the Hawaiian group left, we trooped down to the auditorium where over 1,200 people were waiting for the open lecture. Emma was on my arm as we settled into the seats in the first row at the center.

The next day when the class started with some 800 in attendance, in order not to make the ladies feel self-conscious, Joel did not attend their lectures; so for the next couple of days I would shuttle back and forth between the women's talks and Joel's suite letting him know how they were doing.

At the final meeting, Joel himself spoke to the group. He was more sentimental than usual as he pointed out what a miracle the Infinite Way had been. He looked down to the front row where I was sitting, and for the first time in public Joel recalled how I had read the introduction to *The Infinite Way* over van Druten's shoulder as he was writing it.

That afternoon after the class ended, Joel and I sat

alone in his suite. We lapsed into meditation for a bit, and when we opened our eyes he said, "If I live long enough I will take the Infinite Way beyond healing." At that time I didn't recognize the significance of his statement. Later I realized he did not mean that healings would not be included in the lives of those who followed the Infinite Way, but that we would no longer specifically ask for healings knowing that they would automatically take place when God was experienced.

We sat in silence for a short while after which Joel suddenly asked, "Walter, why don't I have any male teachers?" I remembered what had happened to Floyd with his group on Maui when Joel would come in and dominate, and why I did not want to put myself in the same situation; so I thought "Because there is only one cock in the barnyard." However, the time had passed to get into that discussion, and I didn't want to hurt Joel by implying that there had been anything lacking in him, his teaching, or his guidance; so I shook my head as a noncommittal answer. I remember thinking that women are good at raising up children, and as the Infinite Way was Joel's child it was appropriate that the women teachers he had designated would maintain the purity of his message.

Joel then asked me, "Walter, when are you going to teach?" Again, I didn't want to upset Joel, but I had to express what I felt and said, "Joel, I will never teach the Infinite Way. I can't! Only you can. I can only teach whatever my consciousness is. But I will always answer any call that comes, and I will always say that what I have was built on the foundation that I received from my teacher, Joel Goldsmith." Joel jumped up from his chair, shook my hand, and said over and over "Thank you, thank you, thank you," as much as to say, "Thank God someone has heard me." He knew that his work with me had brought me to the place where I had to, and could, live by my inner contact with my own higher consciousness. That, in turn, was the end goal Joel wanted for all who came to the Infinite Way.

When I left Joel, I went down to the lobby of the hotel and had an experience I will never forget. From one end of the Statler Hotel to the other was a wide hall or passageway. As I entered, there were throngs of people going in both directions, and I felt something I had not ever quite felt before. As I looked at the faces, I saw myself in all of them and I kept thinking, "There I go, there I go." I was experiencing the infinite I AM that is within everyone, and a great love for all humankind filled my soul. To me everyone was the presence of God.

That night I took Joel and the six women across the street to a fine dining room in the Gladstone Hotel as my guests. Joel sat at one end of the table and I at the other with the women on either side. We toasted our love with champagne and followed with the chef's best. There was great joy, and someone said, rather prophetically, "This is the last supper," and, indeed, it was the last time we were all together. As we crossed the street going back to the hotel, Joel and I walked arm-in-arm. The feeling of love and the warmth between us was so intense that even today I can close my eyes and live it again. I realize it signified a kind of completion to our 18-year human/spiritual sojourn. The next day we all left. Emma, Daisy, and a dozen others went off with Joel to London and I went down to Texas to visit my mother in San Antonio.

Ten days later at around dusk, my mother sent me to the grocery store for something. Mother's home was on a hill and as I pulled out of the driveway I saw a magnificent double rainbow, the kind you see often in Hawaii but seldom in Texas. I was overwhelmed with a feeling of the rainbow's significance and stopped the car to meditate for a few minutes.

The next morning when I woke up I told mother that I felt I was now to start putting things down on paper, and just as I finished telling her that, the phone rang with a call telling me that Joel had passed on. Somehow, I have never had a sense of death or discontinuity where what is called death is concerned. Even when my mother died I felt sorry for the vacancy her leaving made in my life, but not for her going to another dimension.

When I heard that Joel had gone all I felt was that he had accomplished what he came to do and now had entered a new phase. I realized that with the time difference between London and Texas, Joel had passed on shortly after the time I saw the rainbow.

On his final night in London, Joel dined with Emma, Lorraine, and Eugene Exman, his New York editor. At dinner Joel was in high spirits and spoke with a kind of urgency as though he was compelled to say everything that was on his mind that night. He apologized for having dominated the conversation, and when he finished he just as suddenly excused himself and went to his room. Without explaining to Emma just why, he asked her to call the hotel physician to look him over. Everything checked out all right. He and Emma went to sleep. Emma told me that sometime later on she heard a rushing sound come from Joel like the expulsion of a full breath, and he was gone.

The morning after Joel died the employees at the Piccadilly Hotel in London where he was staying were surprised and confused by the conduct of his followers. Though their beloved teacher had just died, his students were running around the hotel laughing and full of joy. Instead of being sorrowful over his death, they were celebrating his life.

After Joel was cremated, Emma left London and returned to Hawaii with his ashes, and to this day, according to his instructions, no one knows where they are interred. Joel always thought of Maui as his spiritual home, and I believe that is where he wanted them placed.

CHAPTER TEN

# Joel After Joel

Joel may have physically left this human plane of existence, but the consciousness he represented and symbolized remains in force. When Joel spoke of the "inner work" and that there would come a time when a teacher might be more effective from the "other side," he didn't mean that a personality called Joel Goldsmith would be flying around in space influencing people's lives. Joel was a state of consciousness—a state of consciousness known as the Infinite Way. To the degree that students of the Infinite Way assimilate and are affected by that consciousness, it continues to work in, through, and on them. What's more, as that consciousness continues to grow and expand beyond where Joel left it, those who are of that consciousness also continue to expand and grow.

As for myself, I had several different feelings about Joel's passing. I felt a great loss at not having direct access to the spirit and revelations that came from Joel personally, and I also felt a slight fear that those revelations might not continue at all without his presence. I felt very keenly the personal loss of a father that I could turn to, and yet another part of me felt a kind of release. For so many years I had wanted Joel's approval, while also simultaneously fearing his rejection, almost always afraid that I would not live up to his expectations. Now that he was gone, I felt there was no one remaining whose spiritual judgments could intimidate me or make me feel inferior.

It was not long, however, before I received a clear sign of Joel's continuing influence in my life. I was still involved with the fabric printing factory in Key West, and I had to make a quick two-day trip to New York to deliver some fabrics for a photo shoot. When I arrived in New York I tried to find a room in the usual hotels I frequented, but I found that a national automobile show was going on and all the hotels were full. Before continuing my search, I caught a taxi to go back to the airport to pick up the fabrics which had come on a later flight.

As the taxi was passing the Savoy-Plaza Hotel on the corner of 58th and Fifth Avenue, my intuition kicked in and it said for me to try there; so I stopped the taxi, told the driver I had changed my mind, and marched confidently into the hotel. At the reservation desk I looked the clerk in the eye and announced, "You have a room for me!" He did a double take and said, "All right, we've just had a checkout but the room won't be ready for an hour." I registered and took another taxi to the airport.

Later, as I walked back into the hotel, I suddenly remembered that Adela Rogers St. Johns stayed at the Savoy-Plaza when she was in New York. When I dropped my bags off in my room I called her up. Adela answered the phone and exclaimed, "Walter, this is a miracle. Come to my suite right away." I hurried up to her rooms and after the usual greetings she told me why she felt my being there was a miracle. She said that she was two-thirds of the way through writing the most important novel of her career, and that she had been stuck for months and couldn't finish the book. She said that she hadn't let anyone read what she had written up to this point, not even her agent or editor, but she felt that my arrival was by divine intention and that if I would read what she had written I might find a solution to her blockage.

Unfortunately, I was only to be in the city for one night and the next day, and I had important dinner plans for that evening. Just as I was starting to explain this to Adela the phone rang, and as the Spirit would have it, the call was from my dinner date canceling our meeting. Adela called room service to order some dinner for us while she explained what she wanted the book to say. After dinner I went to my room and stayed up into the night reading her manuscript.

The next morning, in meditation I "heard" or intuited a possible solution, and returned to Adela's suite with the suggestion. I then went about my business during the day, and when I returned that afternoon Adela had an outline of the last third of the novel written on pages stuck on the walls all around the room with scotch tape. She was overcome with excitement and gratitude.

We had a glass of wine to celebrate, and during the conversation she told me that Joel had been her practitioner on the book, that she had asked him to keep her and it in his prayers. I asked her how long ago she had become stuck and couldn't finish the book. She said, "Just about three months ago." "Adela," I replied, "Joel died three months ago." She hadn't realized the connection, but when I came to the hotel her contact with someone in the Infinite Way consciousness was re-established and the words flowed through her again.

That novel, *Tell No Man*, was Adela St. Johns' most successful book. When it was published she sent me a copy with an inscription on the first page: "For Walter—In memory of the night when you solved the blockage so that I could finish this book! We both had a lot of help, I know, but it is a joy to put my gratitude in the book, which came from the manuscript you read then—With my deepest love, Adela Rogers St. John."

A year or two later, Adela returned the favor in a remarkable way. What took place then set the direction for my whole future life.

Once I had moved full-time to Key West, I only made brief trips to New York. This year, however, my inner guidance told me that there was an important reason for me to return and spend at least two months there. When I arrived old friends welcomed me with a spate of parties and dinner engagements, but before long I was left on my own again, and I felt I was floundering with no real purpose for my life. I believed it was now time to start some kind of spiritual work, but still had no clue as to what it would be. Having lost my appetite for a social life, I would often go sit in St. Patrick's Cathedral on Fifth Avenue, trying to open myself for direction.

One afternoon I was having tea with Adela in her suite when she surprised me by saying, "Walter, you have to write a book about Joel. They are idolizing him and putting him on a pedestal. He never wanted that to happen. You knew him better than anyone else; so you should tell his story." I protested, "Adela, I am not a writer. I'm 45 years old, I don't know how to write, and it's too late to learn. Moreover, my guidance doesn't tell me to try."

Adela continued to insist, and a week or so later something extraordinary happened that caused me to change my mind. I was invited to a dinner party in Gramercy Park for Eudora Welty, the Southern novelist, Sidney Kingsley, a famous playwright of that time, his movie actress wife, and Martha Graham, the mother of American modern dance. I arrived, we had wine, and waited for Martha. Finally the dinner was about to get cold; so the host served it and we all sat down to eat. Just as we did, Martha, who was a personal student of Carl Jung's and was the most highly respected choreographer in the entire dance world, arrived three sheets to the wind. By that I mean she had obviously had a great deal to drink and wasn't interested in eating.

Martha's arriving in that condition had the strangest impact on me. I didn't know that St.-Martha-of-the-dance had that little problem, but what I saw from it was that the larger the lip of the funnel, the greater the pressure on the spout. To the degree that infinity pours through an individual, it has impact on the finite vehicle or personality. Many would like to be a Martha Graham, a Tennessee Williams, or a Joel Goldsmith, but few are willing to pay the price of having that much power pouring through their human frame.

I also saw that the finite has to diminish before the infinite. At face value no finite thing can fully express infinity. This is symbolized by Jesus, the finite man, dying on the cross in order to reveal his infinite nature.

What I saw that night had a powerful effect on my life. It made me put aside my personal sense of ego, of what I thought I could or could not do. I saw that it may be wrong to try and yank doors open, but it is worse to refuse to go through the doors that do open to see what is on the other side, and Adela's suggestion was an opened door. As the result of what I saw that night, I said, "All right, God. I will try to write a book."

I could see that there were several purposes in my trying to write. First, putting one's thoughts on paper is a kind of spiritual catharsis. Second, I realized that in response to some of my ideas many of my sophisticated friends had asked me what they could read. I knew that if what I gave them to read smacked of traditional religion and Bible quotes they would be put off. Also, I saw there was no way I could tell them to read particular parts of a number of different books. The third reason was that I didn't feel I could suggest they read Joel's books, fearing they wouldn't be able to get beyond his spiritual sounding language; so if I was to write I would have to do so in a way that would put his principles in modern language, avoiding metaphysical terminology. I concluded that perhaps the time had indeed come for me to write my own book, have a vanity press publication, and print out a few copies to give to friends at my own expense.

All the following year I tried to write. What I did get down on paper was amateurish, awkward, and sterile. When I let my friend James Leo Herlihy, author of *Midnight Cowboy*, read it, he told me very bluntly to forget it. Meanwhile, during that same year my public work began to take shape, and I was asked to give a number of lectures. They were taped and then transcribed.

At the end of the year I was once more in New York and gave Adela the transcribed lectures to read. She called me the very next day, and said that there were a number of good ideas in my talks, but that they needed to be written rather than spoken. I reminded Adela that I didn't know how to write, and she said that if I would come to her suite on Thursday afternoon she would plot out a structure for me to work with. In what turned out to be another divine synchronicity, Adela was staying in the Dorset Hotel this year instead of the Savoy-Plaza.

When I arrived, Adela was pacing back and forth in her suite. She immediately said, "I was wrong. You do have to write a book, but not about Joel. You have to write what the Spirit tells you to write. I was also wrong in telling you that we could work out a structure. You have to write from spirit." Still pacing back and forth, Adela continued excitedly, "Last night something amazing happened to me. I was visited by the ghost or spirit of John van Druten, and he told me to tell you that he will help you write that book."

The hair on the back of my neck stood up and a shiver traveled down my spine! John always stayed at the Dorset when he was in New York and I remembered that just before he died he lived in the suite right below Adela's. But more importantly, at that instant I realized something about the continuity of consciousness.

I had worked closely with John for over twelve years, and even though he lived in California and I lived in New York, we had written to each other at least once a week. I tried to match his style in my letters, and by doing so I was to some degree tuning into his writer consciousness just as I had tuned into Joel's spiritual consciousness. I had contributed to and worked alongside John while he wrote his plays, and had read everything he had ever published. By osmosis I had assimilated his writer consciousness at a level from which I could write. Because his consciousness was at work in mine, you could say that John, too, was working from the invisible. So, I wrapped things up in New York and immediately went to my house in Key West to give it a try.

At first I couldn't get started, but then something came to me in meditation that freed me up. My inner voice said that whenever someone was dependent for their own good on another person, job, or business for fulfillment,-they are psychically hooked up to that person or situation. Although I was no longer actually working in the silkscreen business, I still owned 25 percent of the company, and as my partners had very different spiritual principles than I and were indulging in some business practices that I didn't approve of, it was time for me to break the connection. I knew that I would not receive anywhere near the value of my stock if I sold out to them, but I followed my orders and did so anyway for a fraction of the company's true value.

On the morning we closed on the sale, I hopped on my bike (bicycles were the primary means of transportation in Key West in those days) to return home. As I passed the town book store, on a sudden impulse I went inside to look around. Lying on the counter in plain view was a copy of *Variety*, the weekly theater trade publication. I picked it up to see what was going on in New York, and right on the front page was an announcement that the producer, Hal Prince, had bought the rights to *I Am a Camera* and planned to make it into a musical called *Cabaret*.

As an example of how the spirit works, to this day I get royalties from productions of *Cabaret*, which continues to have revivals. By following my inner orders telling me to sell my interest in the fabric company, even though it seemed that I was putting my future financial status in jeopardy, I ended up receiving, from the musical, many times what my stock would have been worth if I had kept it. Miraculously, every time I have had a particular financial need, such as the funds to develop my retreat center, a new production of *Cabaret* comes about, and my needs are more than fulfilled. God works in mysterious ways.

The next revelation that gave me the key that allowed me to begin writing had to do with the spiritual diaries I kept during my years of study with Joel. The diary entries were what I called my "clicks," those times when I experienced a truth at an inner level. I always kept the entries short, concise, and to the point. No rambling. My guidance instructed me to go through the diaries and put each of the separate ideas on an individual index card. I did so and ended up with a stack of cards five inches high. I then sorted through the cards, arranged them in a kind of continuity, and simply peeled off the first one, elaborated on it, and continued. In ten days I had a first draft.

The morning I started writing the book, a little kitten appeared out of nowhere on my terrace. Because he was solid white from head to toe I started calling him Snowdrop. From that day on I had to keep Snowdrop out of the room where I was working, because he would spring up onto the typewriter almost as if he was trying to help me write. On the evening that I finished the first draft of the book, I was meditating when Snowdrop jumped up on my lap and settled in. While stroking the cat, I was shocked when I suddenly remembered that in van Druten's autobiography he had said that when he was a child he was nicknamed "Snowdrop" because he had a fondness for the flowers of that name that bloom in England in the spring. It made me feel that John's consciousness, if not presence, had indeed helped me write the book. The next day the cat disappeared as suddenly as it had arrived.

Thinking that I would simply get a few copies printed for my friends, I let several people read the manuscript. The reactions were more than encouraging, and several said it ought to be published. Without using an agent, I sent the manuscript to Harper & Row, publisher of Joel's books and the most prominent religious publishers of the time. To my delight, within a week I got a call from a senior editor saying they wanted to publish it. He asked if I would come to New York and work on it with him. I checked into a suite at the Fifth Avenue Hotel and began daily sessions with my editor.

As often happens, the publishers didn't like the title I had chosen, and told me that they had to have a new one over the weekend because the catalogue of upcoming books was going to press the next week. I was reading Tielhard de Chardin's *The Divine Milieu,* and in it there was a prayer that said, "...lay hold on me fully, both by the Within and the Without of myself, grant that I may never break this double thread of my life." There it was, *The Double Thread,* a much more suitable title, the real essence of that book, and the theme of all the books I have written since. Harper & Row's accepting that first book pushed me into a whole new way of life.

I now found myself in what should have been an exhilarating position; my book was being published by the most respected religious publisher in the English language, but, in fact, I was miserable. After reading an advance copy I felt sure the writing was naive and unreadable. I had no idea who would buy my book because I had no following at all and no platform from which to speak. My guidance had told me not to use the Infinite Way mailing list to promote it and I couldn't think of any other audience.

I sat down in the Church of Saint Mary the Virgin on 46th Street off Broadway, the church known as "Smoky Mary's" because of its solemn, dark interior that reeks of frankincense and myrrh. Tears ran down my face and I felt lost and miserable. Despite the fact that on the cover of my book was a quote from Tennessee Williams saying, "With simple and deeply personal eloquence, Walter Starcke explores for us a way out of and above the final world of materialism," I doubted that anyone would read it and wondered why Harper & Row had published it to begin with.

If I needed further proof that something other than myself was in charge of my life, I got it the next day. The day after my desperation in Smoky Mary's, I got a call from a Unity minister named Sig Paulson who was the chaplain at

Unity's world headquarters in Missouri. Sig had been sent an advance copy of *The Double Thread* by the publishers and called them to find my number. Many years before, when he was in the business world, Sig had heard Joel speak in Seattle and had wanted to become an Infinite Way practitioner, but because there was no formal organization and no official ordinations he decided to become a Unity minister. Eventually, Sig became the minister of the Unity church in New York City on Fifth Avenue. During the years that Joel gave classes in New York, whenever someone wanted to get married or there was a need for a licensed minister, we would go to Sig's church.

Presently Sig was organizing the first-ever conference on "Healing the Whole Man" at Unity Village in Missouri. He had invited 29 of the metaphysical movement's major leaders and had space for one more participant. After reading my book he called me at the last minute and invited me to attend the conference.

I accepted, but felt woefully in over my head. This was the first time I had ever been involved in any activity of this nature apart from assisting at Joel's meetings. I arrived at Unity Village on a Sunday afternoon in June; the conference was to start the next day. When I was shown my room I was informed that every Sunday evening in the summer there was a talk in the amphitheater and that I could attend if I wanted. Having nothing else to do I went to the impressive open-air amphitheater where several hundred people were in attendance and I was handed a program. When I took my seat I looked at it and was shocked to see that the title of the speaker's message was "The Double Thread." I didn't realize that it was about "my" *Double Thread* and thought that somehow the speaker had had come up with the same title that I had.

The speaker that night was Dr. Ernest Wilson, an icon of the Unity movement who was the minister at the impressive Unity Temple in Kansas City. This charming little man with his broad smile came to the podium and began by saying, "I keep a stack of books by my bed that publishers send me. Before going to sleep I take a look at one of them, and by a page or two I know what the book is going to say and put it aside, but last night I was up all night reading this one. It was like hearing myself think. It was *The Double Thread* by Walter Stark (not pronouncing my name "star-key")."

I felt as though the heavens opened up and a shaft of light pierced my being! This was the very first response I had from anyone other than my publisher and Tennessee Williams. I went backstage afterwards and introduced myself to Wilson, who was surprised and pleased to meet me. Of course he hadn't known I would be there. We became good friends and I spoke for him at the temple several times after that.

My appearance at that conference launched me on a path that I had always felt would be mine one day but had begun to doubt. I met the top leaders of the metaphysical movement, and several of them asked me to speak at their churches. From nowhere I was now right in the middle of a public work, and my book was soon in its second printing.

Over the next six years I was not involved with any business activities and concentrated on writing and lecturing. I wrote two more books that Harper & Row published, *The Ultimate Revolution* and *The Gospel of Relativity*, which I dedicated to Joel. Towards the end of that period I began to experience strange and unsettling feelings. My meditations were not as spontaneous as they were previously, and I often felt cut off from my inner source. Although I did not realize it at the time, I was entering a classic dark night of the soul, an agonizing condition that lasted off and on for the next two years. I didn't understand my growing anxiety and often felt as though bat wings were beating in my chest. The more I meditated, the worse it got.

My spiritual crisis came to a head when I read a letter written by Joel that Lorraine Sinkler had included in her new book, *The Spiritual Journey of Joel S. Goldsmith*. Before I went down to Virginia Beach to speak for the Edgar Cayce Foundation, the publisher had sent me a copy of Lorraine's book, and my guidance, which is sometimes very specific, told me not to read the book until after I spoke and that I would not understand what it had to tell me until May 6th. That implied that there was something in it that might throw me. There was.

The letter Lorraine had quoted in her book was one Joel had written to her from London months before he died. It shook me and sent me into a state of despair for two reasons: First, because I desperately felt that I needed a healing, and second, because what Joel was experiencing mirrored my own current depression.

Written on November 2, 1963, he said, "This is a critical time for me. I am grieving constantly. I am too 'alone' to bear it, not physically alone but otherwise. And I grieve constantly at my lack. The vision is clear, but somewhere within is an empty space that hurts, pains, and grieves. Tears are never far from my eyes." He said that his spiritual universe had not externalized itself in a harmonious outer world and that his outer universe was as barren as mortal mind itself except that he had a sufficiency of money, and that that was his only sufficiency in the outer picture—"the rest is barren and sad." Then he added, "So I have another notch higher to go. I never dreamed it possible to be so unhappy and survive. It is all such a new experience for me."

In my depressed state, when I read that letter I wanted to throw the book across the room. I felt that if this was what Joel was experiencing before he died, and what I was now feeling, did it mean that after all my years of following his teaching, was that how I was going to end up? Also, it depressed me because Joel always said that we should not expect results in the human scene, and yet his saying his life was barren and sad contradicted that.

I felt many of Joel's students would be confused and upset to hear that Joel went through such a depressed state only six months before he died. I wondered if Lorraine had published the letter in order to prove the extent of her personal relationship with Joel and if she was aware of what she was doing; so I called her to find out. Lorraine told me she had quoted the letter in the book because she felt it would be helpful for Joel's students to know that he also had down periods in his life.

The saving grace of Joel's letter was contained in those final lines, in which he said that this was a new experience for him and that he knew he had "another notch further to go." Joel had been so absolute in closing his mind to the human world that actually facing this depth of depression rather than masking it was perhaps new to him, and his saying that he had another step to go revealed the depth of his spiritual integrity. My guidance had told me that on May 6th I would understand what had taken place and its purpose. In those days I always carried a case of some thirty or so of Joel's taped lectures around with me to play when I needed a lift. On May 6th something told me to open the case of tapes. I pulled one out at random, and was surprised to see that the date on it showed me it was a lecture Joel had given just one week after he had written the letter Lorraine had quoted in her book. I played it and it was like a message from God. It was a tape called *The Two Ways of I*. It became the main thrust of Joel's final year's message, *Between Two Worlds*, and was a link to *The Double Thread*.

It seemed clear to me now that Joel's depressed period was the price he had paid for his next step and final year's work. By his showing us that there are two worlds—one the limited objective world of personal sense, and the other the infinite impersonal subjective world of Spirit—we can close the gap between the two and finally eliminate duality, which is what Jesus intended by giving us two commandments—the instruction to love both the divine and the personal.

# My Dark Night

Seeing that Joel's dark night ended after it had served its purpose was small comfort, because mine was just beginning. Ever since I met Joel and had my first contact in meditation with him I had lived more and more by my intuition, what I call my "guidance." Over the years I relied less and less on my ability to judge right and wrong by human standards, to the point that I didn't have much of a rational mind working for me any more. When the dark night fully took over, my intuition totally cut out on me. It was a nightmare. For the first time in my life I experienced and realized what it must be like to be an average human being living by judgment, always afraid of making the wrong call, and heir to all the fears existential living can produce. I had a hard time with the simplest decisions. I didn't know what can of beans to buy in the grocery store, because I didn't know how to intellectually evaluate which one was better than the other, and the intuition I had lived so totally by heretofore wasn't there to help me.

There was nothing in life I wanted. I had credentials that could open any door, enough fame and fortune to satisfy anyone, and yet life felt empty without my being able to feel God's presence. When I tried to meditate I would often panic. The only reason I didn't seriously contemplate suicide was because at the beginning of my dark period and before my guidance completely cut out on me, it had said that the condition would break on my 54th birthday.

During my dark night, I undertook a 34-city speaking tour when my book, *The Gospel of Relativity*, came out sponsored by the Edgar Cayce Foundation. It was a nightmare. I had to die before every talk to get myself out of the way. When the tour was over, in desperation I returned to my Texas roots and bought a little house on the river in San Antonio. I planted a vegetable garden because, although I couldn't meditate, when I had my hands in the dirt I could feel a little peace.

The day before my 54th birthday, the day my guidance had said my dark night would end, I was digging in the garden when a friend, Jim Smith, came by for a visit. I pulled up a radish, washed it off, and handed it to him. He looked at it and said, "I'm eating dirt." At first I didn't get it, but soon realized that he had seen me plant that little almost invisible seed, and now several weeks later it had transmuted the dirt into this luscious red vegetable.

On my birthday morning, I was once more on the couch in my living room trying to meditate. When I closed my eyes I suddenly pictured an old fashioned railroad sign, "Stop, look, and listen." I did just that. I stopped thinking, looked out at the beautiful trees lining the river across the road from my home, and once more I began to "hear." I thought of Joel and what I heard was, "Walter, you may not be better thân the radish, but you are as good as the radish.

That same life force, that same growth process that has taken place in the radish is taking place in you." I asked, "Then what is wrong?" The first thing the voice said was, "You are still self-centered!"

When I heard I was still self-centered, I realized that it meant I was not so much "self-centered" as "self-conscious." Self-centeredness has a moral connotation, but self-consciousness simply means that when one is self-conscious they are viewing life through the filter of their own personal sense of self or ego, relating everything to one's own being and judgments. Self-conscious people first and foremost see everything in terms of how it relates to them, their personal purpose, and how it affects them; after that they may or may not be aware of the impersonal meaning. Someone can do an important world work and still be self-centered because they are doing it out of a personal need to be of service. A Spirit-centered person who is open to the universe primarily sees how things relate to divine consciousness, and secondly to one's personal sense of self.

After hearing that I was still self-conscious, I asked what I could do about it, and something Eileen Bowden, Joel's favorite student, had said to me came to mind. She had said, "You have to learn instant obedience."

Instant obedience means that the second a poisonous or negative thought enters consciousness, one has to stop it dead in its tracks. As I stated in *The Third Appearance*, we are "thinkaholics." If we do not instantly stop the first thought—drink of negativity—the second one comes easier, and on we go until we are drunk with judgments. We remain poisoned by our minds until we finally sober up.

It took some years to realize what an important breakthrough that experience was for me. It was the key to being able to live the Infinite Way. I paid a heavy price for it, but after that day I was able to use my mind rather than my mind using me as it had so often in the past. I continued having difficulties that I had to handle, but since that time no matter how disturbing a situation is, it takes me no more than a day or two at the most to become free of it and to receive my release from human judgment.

The second important thing I realized from my dark night experience was that I had not been living my own Double-Thread message. I had already written several books and I wouldn't change them today, but I heard them rather than lived them. In my own life I was top heavy on the metaphysical or spiritual side and not equally in tune with the material or human side.

Most people have trouble coming in contact with their divinity or fourth-dimensional awareness. Some people have the opposite problem. They have trouble experiencing the fullness and purpose of their humanity. I was one of those. I thought that I was an ordinary human being. I tried to manipulate life, I had sexual relationships, I cared about making money, and was fairly competitive, but I wasn't actually ever controlled by human desires or human attachments. I never accepted "can't" as a reality. I had always been a loner, like Joel, seldom involved at the personal level with other people. Now I had to learn what it was like to live at the human level of community, how to realistically face up to ordinary human feelings and experiences.

I also realized that I had let myself get out of balance. Once I started writing and lecturing, I had stopped being involved in the business world or in building things and I became too one-sided. To be balanced we need to have both a vocation and an avocation or we need to be involved with activities at the material level and simultaneously with those of a spiritual nature. After all, Jesus was a carpenter and Paul a tent maker.

Shortly before my dark night experience broke, I had visited Fenwicke Holmes, brother to Ernest Holmes, the founder of the Church of Religious Science, and with whom he had co-authored *The Voice Celestial*. At this point the frail Fenwicke was living in a retirement home in Long Beach. As he walked me to my car after our time together, arm in arm, he said, "Walter, I have seen them come and go, all the top leaders, and without exception they have all lost their integrity in the end. You have yours now. Hold on to it."

Integrity means what the word says—integration. We have integrity when our spiritual life and our material life are balanced and integrated, not too much emphasis on either level. That way we close the gap between the divine and the human.

Everything at the material level eventually loses its integrity. Our bodies die and end up in ashes or a grave. Fortunately, we have bodies, but we are not bodies, so we don't have to worry about them finally disintegrating. Even rocks lose their rock integrity and finally crumble. Eventually some teachers loose their integrity because they begin to believe that their teachings are necessary; otherwise they wouldn't teach to begin with. The more that people tell their teachers they have been helped by their message, the more the teacher is tempted to personalize and believe that it is their own message.

Shortly after my meeting with Fenwicke, my dark night ended and I knew what I had to do. I had to go on a long retreat from public work. I realized that it wasn't a matter of my always having perfect integrity. It was a matter of my holding on to it as long as I could, and I couldn't do that if I continued only writing and talking.

Knowing that the time had come for me to follow Fenwicke's advice, I bought a ranch outside of San Antonio on the Guadalupe River, started a community of young artists, and retreated from public work. I remained at the ranch for 14 years without any public lecturing, traveling, or writing.

Finally, my old editor from Harper & Row, who had retired, visited his daughter in San Antonio and came out to see me. He saw what I had been putting into my computer and told me that I should write another book. I told him that I wasn't out to change the world and didn't miss writing books or lecturing. He said that if I would write again he would edit it, and as he was the best of all possible editors, it seemed like a sign; so I wrote *Homesick for Heaven, you don't have to wait!* That pushed me back out into the public eye after 14 years of silence. *Homesick* was followed by *It's All God,* which required a study guide as a number of churches began to teach it as an eight-week course. *The Third Appearance,* the book that preceded this one, marries science to mysticism and is less scriptural than the others.

I continue to write, travel, lecture, and be involved simultaneously with the business world. It isn't that I think that I have "the" answer or that I want to save the world. I don't believe that it needs saving. Though we may not understand what is going on, and may not consciously be aware that God is the only power, everything that is taking place is right on time for this stage in the evolution of our collective consciousness. On the other hand, when I see people hitting their thumb with a mental hammer and screaming in pain, I want to say, "Stop, you don't have to do that."

After I began to lecture around the country I became more and more concerned about some responses I heard to Joel's writings. Though I have received many letters from people saying that because of my references to Joel they have read him and want to thank me, an even greater number have come to me and said that because of my books they are now able to understand the Infinite Way and make it work for them.

A considerable number of people have turned their back on Joel's message because of a couple of key issues or because he worded things in a way that to them has clouded his true meaning. I hated to see people denying themselves the invaluable blessing in 98 percent of what Joel had to say because of the two percent that was confusing them and needed reinterpretation in order for it to fulfill its promise.

I am absolutely convinced that if Joel were alive today he would explain a few things differently, less scripturally and more in the language of the present day. By doing so he would clear up the confusions inherent in his, and in most, theology. I feel that I know what Joel really meant, despite some of the language he used that complicates understanding today.

By the same token, I believe that when Joel was speaking he gave his message at the level that the collective consciousness could assimilate at that time, a level that was more traditional than today's. That is why I decided to write this book, restate some of his key issues, and point out what were, for me, some stumbling blocks and how I got around them.

Walter in his Key West house, 1960.

Walter during early writing years, 1969

CHAPTER ELEVEN

# Conclusions

$\mathcal{J}$esus didn't give us the "final word" as many claim. He gave us the "first word." We honor him as the one who first introduced Christ consciousness to our world. After his physical presence was no longer on Earth, the Christ message that Jesus initiated continued to not only enhance the lives of those who endeavored to live it, but the consciousness he brought forth has also continued to grow, expand, and evolve beyond where he left it, as he said it would—"greater works shall ye do."

Similarly, we honor Thomas Edison as the father of electricity because he invented the first simple light bulb. It was a far cry from the powerful laser beams we use today; nevertheless, Edison's initial principle remains the basis of today's most advanced technologies. Similarly, Jesus' I AM vision is the source of Western mysticism and metaphysics today.

When Joel wrote to John van Druten that there would be a time when he would work more effectively from the inner plane, he didn't mean that he as a person named Joel would be flying around getting into people's heads. Rather, he talked about the impersonal nature of his Infinite Way consciousness and the mistake orthodox churches made in personalizing and deifying Jesus, the teacher, rather than honoring and emphasizing his message.

Joel was a state of consciousness, and that consciousness continues to enlighten and heal us, though I and others have added to and reinterpreted it in terms of today's language. If one subscribes to Carl Jung's belief that ideas continue to expand even after their initiator has died, Joel's consciousness is progressively growing and expanding until it will reach its fulfillment. That may include additional ideas and interpretations presented by a number of different people who have assimilated his consciousness and come up with workable concepts that were not necessarily voiced by Joel when he was on Earth. It may also mean re-wording some of the Infinite Way principles in a language that is more easily understood today, and one that has a broader interpretation.

Personally, when I say that I feel Joel's presence or that Joel speaks to me, what I mean is that I am aware of the state of consciousness that came into the world as Joel, and there are times when I experience that presence so vividly that a sense of his human personality is present with me as well.

When Joel said that he was going to take the Infinite Way beyond healing, he was lifting his belief into a different dimension, one where we need not pray or do mental work. He was saying that if we lived through our higher consciousness, everything would take care of itself naturally without words or our trying to make it happen. It certainly has for me! With little more than starting each day with a deep sense of gratitude for the divine process at work in my life, everything in my life falls into place—perhaps not always just when I think it should but always before long and often in unexpected ways. Certainly, new challenges come up but the solutions trail not far behind.

If I look at my life in personal terms I have to admit that this Infinite Way consciousness works. At past 85 I have only temporary physical complaints. I walk and jog with my dog up to a mile a day and have plenty of energy, financial abundance, an enjoyable home in San Antonio, and another on the beautiful Guadalupe River in the Hill Country outside of the city. I am blessed with some devoted companions who are aware of and lovingly accept my humanity without losing sight of my divinity, particularly with my partner of twenty-six years, Eron Howell. She is a constant inspiration, organizes my seminars, and manages most of my business affairs. To top it off, at the turn of the century the International New Thought Alliance honored me with what they called "The Mystic Century Award." What more could anyone want?

For over 40 years I felt that my continued silence about Joel's and my relationship was called for; however, when Catherine Ponder suggested that the time had come for me to share our personal experiences, I meditated for guidance. Finally, I came to the conclusion that if I pointed out some of the stumbling blocks that I had encountered along the way and how I resolved them, it might be of value for others who faced the same dilemmas.

There is one major difference between Joel and me—Joel never studied the Infinite Way. He didn't have to because he gave birth to it. As a student I had to find ways to make the principles work for me individually. Right from the beginning I sensed the truth in the message, and I often felt something was wrong with me because I failed to achieve the results or the experiences that it promised. Over the past 60 years, by trial and error, I have stumbled on some "how tos" that have helped me realize the full potential inherent in the Infinite Way. I am ready to share them because, in the end, what I discovered eliminated any lingering doubts and replaced them with confirmation.

It is important to remember that we live in a different world than the one Joel addressed 50 years ago. The seeds that were planted in consciousness at that time have been bearing fruit since then, and as a result we are not in the same place that we and the metaphysical world were then.

For example, as I reported earlier, Joel always instructed us that after his tapes were played at meetings, there shouldn't be any discussion and that everyone should leave in silence. That may have been appropriate then, because few students had worked with his teaching long enough to fully grasp its full significance, and discussions might have led to confusion. Today, however, if those who have been involved with Joel's teaching for years cannot help clarify confusions and point out important subtleties in discussion groups, then something is lacking in either the teaching or in us.

A true message does not change over time. However, different times demand that the emphasis be placed on different areas or stages of development as one progresses. I haven't found any of my beliefs that are not corroborated by Joel somewhere in one or another of his writings. I would not attempt to offer any suggestions or the "how tos" that have helped me if I did not feel that I know and have experienced Joel's consciousness and have been aware of the problems he faced introducing his absolute mysticism to the divided collective consciousness that he confronted in his time.

# Mystical Confusion

Joel's message is alive today because of his uniquely inspired mysticism and the spiritual experience it induces, not because of his metaphysics or because of the human disciplines that at one time or the other he says we have to follow in order to become illuminated. Clarity comes when we are aware of those times when Joel is outlining the human steps and not confuse those steps with the all-important mystical experience they are designed to lead us to.

For instance, over and over I would be lifted into higher consciousness when Joel told me, "Ye are now the son of God," "You are all that God is," or "That which you are seeking you already are." Then later, I would become confused when he said, "Ye are the sons of God when you experience God consciousness." I didn't know whether I already was the son or whether I would be at some future time. However, when I was able to consciously differentiate between those times when he was outlining the metaphysical exercises needed to get me to the experience of my higher consciousness and when he was telling me of my true being, confusion departed and Joel's mysticism became a present reality. All teachings, bar none, have that problem. They all imply that if you follow their instructions you will become something in the future that you are not already being. When you accept the belief that you are not already the presence of God, limitations become self-fulfilling prophecies.

When Gautama the Buddha received enlightenment he said, "To one who has arrived the way is foreign," meaning that all the steps that one takes to become enlightened no longer appear reasonable or necessary once one has reached illumination. Out of his passionate desire to help us arrive at that experience, Joel spent the greatest amount of his time explaining the journey that personal sense goes through in order to arrive; however, those rarer moments when he offers his absolute mysticism are the heart and life of his message. When I became consciously aware of the difference between those times that he was talking to me as a human being on the journey, and no longer confused them with those times when he was addressing the I that I AM, perplexity was replaced by an actual experience of my divinity.

Lorraine Sinkler, Joel's editor, must have been aware of this problem because she had the publisher italicize his meditations and those passages where he was unequivocally voicing his pure mysticism. If one reads only the italicized parts of his books, a clear picture of his mystical vision emerges.

# The Thirteenth Step

In most religions anything that has to do with one's acknowledging the presence of God is referred to as mysticism. Joel took mysticism beyond theory and made it experiential. He made it the thirteenth step. Until then religions and the evolution of our individual spiritual journeys have taken us through progressive stages similar to those that Alcoholics Anonymous has outlined in its twelve steps. The Twelfth Step is the one where a person takes responsibility for doing God's work in the world. Joel takes us into The Thirteenth Step - the mystical experience where all duality is eliminated, where there is no God "and" us. At the Thirteenth Step we "are" the presence of God. We do not do God's work—we are the embodiment of God's work.

# The Impossibility of Absolutes

For years the scripture, "Be ye therefore perfect, even as your Father which is in heaven is perfect," was for me a major stumbling block and a fountain of guilt. I confused spiritual perfection with the mores of human conduct and constantly blamed myself for not being able to absolutely live them. Finally I realized that absolutes do exist in theory and are the ultimate truth, but at the less-than-absolute level of my human existence they do not exist. There is never a "never" or always an "always." When I saw that absolute truth does exist subjectively at the impersonal level of fourth-dimensional consciousness, but not objectively at the level of my third-dimensional personality, it took a load of self-judgment off of my consciousness. I saw the value of aiming at absolutes without having to blame myself when I did not achieve them.

Absolutes exist at the ascension level, but when we reach that level we no longer exist physically. Until then, the virtue of aiming at absolutes is that by aiming at them, we come closer to achieving them than we would have if we hadn't tried to achieve them. We should be idealists aiming at absolutes rather than perfectionists always feeling failures for not being able to humanly live them.

Eventually I found that my human imperfections were my perfection, because they kept me seeking to live by my higher consciousness. After all, Jesus, too, was perfect, but not flawless. He stumbled, he fell, he cried, and even contradicted himself, but he was perfectly what a growing, evolving human being can be. As I said earlier, this side of his ascension Jesus said, "Touch me not for I have not ascended," meaning humanly he was still at the level of personal sense where absolutes do not exist.

Joel repeated that he was not an absolutist, but coming out of Christian Science he carried over a number of absolute statements that we have to be aware of, absolutes that I am sure he would not advocate in the same way today.

For example, I felt confused because I would have what I thought was an experience of the presence of God and then I would read Joel's absolute statement, "Once you experience the presence of God, never again will you feel alone." Then later when I had a bout of loneliness I begin to doubt that what I thought was my experience of God was real. The truth is that I was never alone because God was there whether I experienced it or not. I just wasn't aware of it at that moment. I had truly experienced the presence of God, but at those temporary times when I was not in my higher consciousness I felt alone just as Joel did when he wrote Lorraine of his loneliness a few months before he died.

Joel wrote, "There is always [absolute] the sense of an inner companionship." Now when I read that statement I replace "always" with "mostly," and take comfort in the fact that most of the time I feel the presence of an inner companion. When I hear, "I of my own self can do nothing," it becomes more inclusive if I think, "I of my own self 'alone' can do nothing," because I can do all things when I am in my higher consciousness.

I continued to believe that I was not a good example of an accomplished Infinite Way student until the end of Joel's life when he went beyond absolute statements by introducing the subject of living between two worlds—not absolutely one or the other. Then when I read in *The Infinite Way,* "We have been concerned with the letter of truth, now only with the spirit of truth," I realized that Joel wasn't being absolute and excluding the letter of truth or he wouldn't have attempted to give it to us because we operate at both the spiritual and human levels. It would have sounded less contradictory if he had said that as human beings, "We have been concerned with the letter of truth, now also or primarily [not only] with the spirit of truth." The letter of truth is a necessary complement to the spirit of truth, one third-dimensional and the other fourth-dimensional.

When I read on page 21 of *Practicing The Presence*, "There is no longer [absolute] any concern as to whether we are rich or poor, sick or well," I was confused because both Joel and Jesus were concerned enough to heal and supply their followers. There is nothing wrong with having human concerns as long at they do not imply that one believes in a power apart from God. I have never met anyone yet who did not have some form of concern even if it is to impart truth.

Absolutes do exist beyond personal sense and we can have the benefit of Joel's teaching and avoid confusion by "double thinking"; thus we can be constantly alert to the truth of being at those times when he makes absolute statements, and at the same time not confuse them with our human expectations.

# Double Think

"Double Think" is a term I borrowed from George Orwell's *1984*. It helped me solve the paradox of having to deal with a "me" that is and a "me" that is my concept of who I am. For many years I felt I was a failure because I couldn't make my humanity be spiritual no matter how hard I tried. Finally there came a time when I realized that if I really concentrated I could think several different things simultaneously without mushing them together like a smoothie to the point that individuality no longer exists. By double thinking I was able to keep individual trains of thought completely separate, and entertain a number of concepts without transposing one on to the other.

I could be aware of my perfect, pure, and present divinity, and I could simultaneously be conscious of my limited third-dimensional personal sense self with its virtues and its faults, and be free of confusion by recognizing from which level I was observing myself.

Just as an actor in a play does not confuse himself with the fictional part he is playing, I started seeing Walter as the fictional part I play on the world stage and that my higher self is the one in the privacy of the dressing room where only those with the capacity to fully love are allowed.

Through double thinking I can consciously know when and to what degree I am seeing myself with the limitations of personal sense, and I can simultaneously be aware that impersonally I am all that God is—complete and whole. Then my human limitations do not become self-fulfilling prophecies and there is no self-deluding contradiction. That doesn't mean that I excuse Walter's faults or let him off the hook. Sometimes I have to discipline him and sometimes I have to nurture him, but always without losing sight of my invisible self that is eternal, and as Joel would say, "Closer than breathing, nearer than hands and feet."

Now when I read Joel's books or listen to his tapes I can double think and be consciously alert to those times when he is addressing my human nature self, and I can value his teaching without losing sight of the absolute perfection that I already am spiritually. When he states that I already am the fullness of the Godhead bodily and he quotes Jesus saying, "Before Abraham was, I am," the perfection of God, I can simultaneously remember who he is talking about at those other times when he says that I have to die daily. By double thinking I can see that the "me" that must die daily is my false sense of self, not the I that I AM.

When I double think, I am one-hundred percent aware that I as Walter can of my own self do nothing, and at the same time I am simultaneously 100 percent aware that when I am in my higher consciousness I can do all things.

# The Virtue of Priority

No sooner did I find a solution for one of my stumbling blocks than another, and perhaps more insidious one, came to light. When I stopped looking for absolutes at the level of personal sense and, through double thinking, was able to become aware of which me I was dealing with at any given time, the divine or the human, the results I wished to achieve were still inconsistent. Once more turning to the two commandments I finally realized the all-important significance of the priority that Jesus outlined.

Jesus said, "The first and great commandment" is the love of God—the spiritual, invisible, or subjective nature of our lives and actions. Elsewhere, he added, "Seek ye first the kingdom of God," which enlists the subjective as the prime priority. I realized that this priority symbolizes the difference between the Old Testament that primarily views life objectively and the New Testament, which advocates a subjective way of life—forgive, judge not, love rather than destroy, punish, or imprison.

I saw that all the problems of my past came about because I had primarily tried to achieve my goals objectively rather than by defining the subjective nature of what I wanted, then following with what I needed to do to objectify my subjective desires.

Then I realized that society in general has also had the cart before the horse. The Christ-conscious message has been misconstrued because governments and individuals have had their priorities reversed. They have thought that a primarily militaristic action or the use of financial pressure rather than altruistic values could produce peace and well-being. It never has.

# The Word Game

On the last page of *The Infinite Way,* Joel's frustration showed itself: "How far have I wandered from Thy Spirit, O Tender One and True, how far, how far! How deeply lost in the maze of words, words, words!" After the umpteenth reading of that passage, I realized what became for me the single most simple, but important, way to close the gap between my divinity and my humanity.

All words are effects. They may convey spirit, but the words themselves are effects. I found that when I learned to live by the Spirit conveyed by the words rather than by their literal interpretation, I was no longer used by them. Now I use the written word, but through double thinking I do not have to be used by it. That includes the words in the Bible as well as the words in all the teachings I have studied. We need to interpret words with a new language—a language of Spirit where we listen to the spirit conveyed by words before hearing their intellectual content.

In the chapter "Demonstrating God" in *Practicing the Presence,* Joel uses the word "God" 162 times in ten pages. Like almost everyone I have ever met, I am so conditioned to think of what God will do for me as though God is something other than myself that it is nearly impossible for me to read or say the word God without consciously or unconsciously thinking that God is other than my own being.

The breakthrough that made it possible for me to fully experience union with my divine consciousness came when I arrived at the point where every time I read or heard the words "God," "Lord," "Master," "Father," "He," "Him," or "It" in Joel's or any other writings, if I constantly and instantly substituted or added "My divine consciousness," or "My higher consciousness" in place of those traditional words, I was free of contradiction. I was so conditioned to think of God as something apart from myself that unless I immediately translated the word into meaning the spiritual truth of my being, I was denying that I was the presence of God, as Joel's mysticism had so eloquently told me.

When Joel wrote me that I was called to mysticism, that my whole being must be filled with "God," he was saying that I was destined to become aware of my "higher consciousness," that my whole being was to be filled with that consciousness. When he said that his consciousness was filled with "God" around the clock, he meant that he was constantly in his higher consciousness.

Now when I repeat the 23rd Psalm, though I may say, "The Lord is my Shepherd. I shall not want. He maketh me to lie down in green pastures," I am thinking, "My higher consciousness is my Shepherd. I shall not want. My consciousness makes me to lie down in green pastures, it leadeth me beside still waters"—and there is no residual sense of separation between myself and my higher consciousness.

When Joel said, "It is His good pleasure to give you the kingdom," the "His" he was referring to is your and my own I AM divine consciousness, not a separate God off in the clouds.

Joel repeatedly said that all is consciousness; therefore, instead of personalizing Jesus' statement, "I am the way, the truth, and the life," when I think of that "I," I think of it as my own divine consciousness being the way, the truth, and the life, and I don't entertain any subconscious duality.

Above all, in my daily meditations when I say, "Speak, Lord, thy servant heareth," Walter is saying, "Speak to me my higher consciousness; thy servant [that part of me that wants to serve the Spirit] heareth."

Once I began to automatically translate the words Joel used so often—Father, Lord, Master, Him, He, and God—as synonyms for my own higher consciousness, my prayers became experiences rather than petitions.

The wonderful thing about substituting "higher consciousness" for the traditional religious words is that when we do, all the spiritual writings from the past that we have valued now come alive in a new and more powerful way. Pick up one of your favorite writings or scriptures and try it. Every time you see the word, God, or any of the other words standing for divinity, believe they are referring to your own divinity.

## The Human Scene

Finally, I have come full circle, back to the main reason I have written this book and included the necessity of double thinking. I know without a doubt that both Joel and his Infinite Way consciousness are at the point in their evolution at which they want this clarification made. Without it omnipresence, omniscience, and omnipotence remain a fiction.

The answer goes back to the revelation I had at the crater on Maui, at which time I saw that the secret of the message of Jesus the Christ was that he gave us two commandments, not just one, and in doing so he avoided either/or and absolutes. He offered us an apparent duality that when reconciled would actually eliminate duality. He told us to love both cause and effect, both the divine and the human, both the subjective principle and the objective result. When we do we will find that they are "like unto each other."

Joel said that revelation is always shocking. It certainly was for me when I realized that all the world's religions have an unresolved paradox. They all include the presence of an all powerful, omnipresent, and omniscient Supreme Being—Brahman, Tao, Allah, or God—and yet they have all created the very duality they say does not exist. By telling us that in order for us to realize our divinity we have to overcome our humanity, lock it in a mental prison, hide it in a monastery, beat it to death with a morality, or subordinate it to a religion or institution, they perpetuate duality. They tell us we have to transcend the testimony of our senses rather than use them to honor God. How could we love ourselves if that is true?

When I told Joel that I would never teach the Infinite Way, it was because I always felt I could not be totally impersonal and eliminate my humanity as long as I had a body. After all, if God, my higher consciousness, created all, then it created my humanity as well as my divinity, illusion or not. My turning point came when I realized that rather than denouncing my humanity—I had to find a purpose for it! After that I was able to experience the fact that it is all God—that what appears are stages of higher consciousness expressed visibly.

I was finally able to come to terms with my dualistic dilemma and fully appreciate that the Infinite Way was truly an infinite way when I realized that the problem wasn't with Joel's message, but rather with the limits of dialectics and the level of consciousness he was addressing when he was present.

When Joel said his breakthrough came when he realized that "God is not in the human scene," he was paraphrasing Jesus, who said that his kingdom was not of "this world." Neither of them meant that God was not present at the material level. They both claimed that the word becomes flesh, and both said that the "Earth is the Lord's and the fullness thereof," and later added, "Son, all that I hath is thine." Both used half-truth language that needed to be complemented by another half truth in order for the whole truth to be expressed. To me, the whole truth is that there is no duality; rather the material scene is how fourth-dimensional consciousness appears at the third-dimensional level, the level of material appearances, but it is all One. It's All God.

Joel was correct in often quoting Paul's statement, "The natural man knoweth not the things of God because they are spiritually discerned." However, it was a freeing moment for me when I realized the other half—that the spiritual man cannot know material things because they are materially discerned. The natural man is not bad, but rather just different. One is fourth dimensional the other third dimensional. Obviously we cannot conceive of the visible in terms of the invisible or the invisible in terms of the visible any more than we can know a particle in terms of a wave or a wave in terms of a particle. They are simply different dimensions of the one divine reality.

In order to live the Infinite Way successfully I found that in studying Joel's writings I had to constantly be aware that when he is talking about humans, the human scene, or personal sense, he is talking about a state of consciousness or ignorance rather than the truth of being. In contrast he would most often say, "God is individual being."

As an example, in the following paragraph Joel makes what could be taken as a demeaning statement about what it means to be a human, and then later he clarifies it:

> *Mortal existence not only is no part of God's kingdom, but cannot even evolve into God's kingdom. Mortal sense and mortal creation have no part in God, never have had, and cannot be returned to God.* *

A few sentences later he clears it up by saying:

> *When we are unclothed of mortality and clothed with immortality there is no fallen man: there is only the original, perfect man, the spiritual identity which is now, and always had been.*

In *Practicing The Presence* Joel says:

> *Spirit is in no way related to the human scene. A spiritual God cannot be brought down to a material concept of life,*

and in *The Contemplative Life:*

> *As human beings we are barren soil, entirely separate and apart from God.*

*Parenthesis In Eternity, p. 136.

Within a few sentences he turns right around and says we should never accept a self-hood apart from God. In either case he was not talking about people but about states of consciousness. We can appreciate both statements and not reject our physical presence if we once more double think and consciously be aware of which reality Joel is talking about when he jumps back and forth.

# The Human Purpose

Until I realized a purpose for my humanity, I couldn't fully love myself. My humanity is a school where I grow my soul. It is a tool that I need in order to accomplish my life's purpose. Just as Michelangelo couldn't sculpt the Pieta out of a piece of marble without a chisel, I need the experiences of my human presence in order to become a conscious being, conscious of my divine reality. My humanity's purpose is for it to be the instrument through which my ignorance is revealed so that I may become conscious and realize my own divine spiritual reality. When I completely attain fourth-dimensional consciousness, I will have graduated from school and no longer manifest in bodily form. There will no longer be any need for my humanity. Every experience and every lesson my human nature has provided has pushed me into waking up; therefore, all of my human experiences have come from my higher consciousness. I wouldn't have studied the Infinite Way to begin with if my need to find a way to cope with my human condition had not pushed me into seeking the truth. In that way, my humanity has been my spirituality expressing itself.

There are no mistakes. My so-called mistakes have led me to my awakening. My humanity has been my greatest blessing, because it has revealed to me how the Spirit operates at the material level. The joy I feel, the abundance I enjoy, and the freedoms I experience are because I now know that IT IS ALL GOD.

Joel's last photo, 3 months before his death.

# Joel's Legacy

*T*he story doesn't end. It is an eternal illustration of the transference and expansion of consciousness that all true mentor relationships encompass. Joel's students are his immortality. He lives on in them and they in him. I often turn to his writitngs and tapes to re-enter his conscousness, and they continue to be a gold mine of inspiration for me. Even when I dip into one of his books at random he continues to teach me, because I discover some subtley I had missed before, and that re-kindles my spirit.

Thank you Joel for your ever-present presence.

The following passage from *The Infinite Way* is repeated at the beginning of every one of his books, and is a portrait of Joel's soul and the gift of freedom he offered the world.

> *Illumination dissolves all material ties and binds men together with the golden chains of spiritual understanding; it acknowledges only the leadership of the Christ; it has no ritual or rule but the divine, impersonal universal Love; no other worship than the inner Flame that is ever lit at the shrine of Spirit. This union is the free state of spiritual brotherhood. The only restraint is the discipline of Soul, therefore we know liberty without license; we are a united universe without physical limits; a divine service to God without ceremony or creed. The illumined walk without fear—by Grace.*

Other books by Walter Starcke:

*The Double Thread*
*The Gospel of Relativity*
*The Ultimate Revolution*
*Homesick for Heaven*
*It's All God*
*The Third Appearance*

for further information about
Workshops, Master Classes, & Retreats,
Newsletters and Speaking Engagements,
contact:
Eron Howell
The Guadalupe Press
P.O. Box 865
Boerne, Texas 78006

or our website:
www.walterstarcke.com

The works of Joel Goldsmith

For information
or to order Joel's tapes contact:

THE INFINITE WAY

P.O Box 2089

Peroia, AZ 85380-2089

or call:

1.800.922.3195


To order Joel's books:

Order through most book stores,
and all are offered through the publisher and distributor,
including those published by Acropolis Books:

DEVORSS & COMPANY

P.O. Box 1389

Caramillo, CA 93011-1389

or call:

1.800.843.5743